THE
REPUBLIC
OF
TEXAS

by Clarence R. Wharton

2021
Copano Bay Press

Originally published in 1922 under the same title.

Design Copyright Copano Bay Press 2021
ISBN 978-1-941324-76-9

PUBLISHER'S DEDICATION

This edition of Wharton's *Republic of Texas* is respectfully and lovingly dedicated to the memory of Michael W. Taylor—devout Aggie, resolute Texan and a dear friend of Copano Bay Press. When the Press was young and trying to find its way, Mike reminded us not to dwell on the problems. Fix them and move on to better things, he told us. "Grind and grow. You'll be fine." We did and (so far) we are.

We take comfort in knowing that Mike has joined the Heavenly chorus where he can swap yarns with Lt. Kyle Drake, a fellow A&M Cadet killed at Iwo Jima before Mike was born, but in whose life we all found kinship.

Thank you for sharing your love of Texas with us, and for sharing our Texana with your family. We'll see you on the other side, Mr. Taylor.

Preface

When the Austins came in 1821 and opened the way for people from the States, Texas history had its real beginning. Fifteen years later San Jacinto was fought and won and for ten years more Texas was a Republic. Then after one of the greatest political battles in American history, it became a state. This twenty-five years is the heroic period of Texas history.

When the Democrats met in convention in Baltimore in 1844, the Whigs had nominated Henry Clay and declared against the annexation of Texas and ignored the acquisition of Oregon. Powerful forces among the Democrats, led by Van Buren and aided by Benton, worked to commit the party to the same course. But the Southern leaders seized the machinery of the convention, overthrew Van Buren, and named James K. Polk, of Tennessee, and boldly declared for the annexation of Texas and the acquisition of Oregon. The election of Polk committed the American people to both propositions. The advent of Texas into the Union was followed not only by all the country west to the Pacific, but North to the present Canadian border. San Jacinto set the tide of Saxon supremacy toward the Pacific and was indeed one of the decisive battles of the world.

CLARENCE R. WHARTON

Houston, Texas
January 1, 1922

I have consulted every work bearing upon Texas History which has ever been published as far as I know, and many original sources of information as well. I desire to make special acknowledgment of material and from valuable information collated by Mr. Justin H. Smith in his elaborate work upon the annexation of Texas published by the McMillan Company in 1919.

C. R. WHARTON

THE COLONIES

FIRST COLONIAL GRANT TO MOSES AUSTIN

January 17, 1921, marked the one hundredth year since the first colonial grant in Texas to Moses Austin. At the beginning of that year Spanish authority still nominally prevailed over Mexico, or New Spain, as it was much called, though the war for Mexican independence had been raging since 1810.

Mexico, which for three centuries had been governed by Spanish viceroys, was a vast country greater in area than any nation of the world save Russia and China. It was divided into twelve Intendencies, the sixth of which was San Luis Potosi, which was itself divided into four provinces and four districts, one of which provinces was Texas. Texas was practically uninhabited except by roving bands of warlike Indians. There were squalid Spanish or Mexican settlements at San Antonio, Nacogdoches, La Bahia and a few other places, remnants of the old missions which had failed.

The seat of government for this province, if it could be so dignified, was at San Antonio, which had been founded nearly a century before. The Spanish policy was one of absolute exclusion of all foreigners. There was considerable doubt about the Spanish title to Texas and this government determined to permit no intrusion by people from the States or elsewhere.

Philip Nolan, who came into Texas in 1812 for the very peaceful purpose of hunting wild horses, was killed by

Spanish soldiers. Such of his comrades as survived were carried into captivity. The Mexican or Spanish people had made no headway in settling here because of the hostility of the Indians, and because there were no rich mines in Texas which would lure the gold hunters who made the first settlements in Mexico, and who later filled California.

In December, 1820, Moses Austin, a native of Connecticut, came on horseback from Washington County, Missouri, where he then resided, and presented himself to the Spanish Governor at San Antonio, seeking permission to found a colony in Texas. He was ordered to forthwith leave the country, and when about to obey this mandatory instruction, he met upon the Military Plaza the Baron de Bastrop, a Belgian soldier of fortune then temporarily in the service of the Spanish government. Bastrop and Austin had met in a restaurant in New Orleans years before and renewed their chance acquaintance upon the Plaza just as Austin was about to resume his long, doleful journey back to the States.

Austin was in fact a Spanish subject, he having been naturalized as such while living in Missouri in 1799, at which date Louisiana, which included Missouri, was under Spanish dominion. Bastrop interceded with the Spanish Governor, and that dignitary being convinced that Austin was not a foreigner accepted his petition for permission to settle three hundred families in Texas. The Governor at San Antonio, however, could not act upon this petition, and on December 26th, 1820, he forwarded it with a letter recommending its acceptance to the Superior Government at Monterey. This memorial was granted by the Spanish authorities at the latter place representing the Supreme Government of the Eastern Internal Provinces of New Spain on the 17th day of January, 1821.

Just what caused the Spanish authorities to revoke their policy of nearly two centuries with reference to allowing foreigners to come into Texas is a matter of much interest. Some students of those times say that it was because there had been a permanent boundary settlement between the United States and Spain at the time of the Florida purchase in 1819, which lead the Spanish authorities to feel that the United States had permanently recognized the Sabine as the boundary between the two countries. Stephen Austin himself stated in after-life that the purpose of the Spanish and Mexican governments in making these grants was to get American colonists into Texas who would reclaim the country from the wild Indians. The vast importance of this event, the granting of this first colonial privilege, one hundred years ago, is not always fully understood. It can be said with much emphasis that it was as important in American history and even in the history of the world as the landing of the Pilgrims at Plymouth two centuries before. It made the way for American colonization and civilization in Texas, and determined that the vast country between the Rio Grande and the Oregon should be Saxon rather than Latin.

Moses Austin started back to the States about January 1st, 1821, going by Natchitoches, Louisiana, where he met his son Stephen. The long journey across this trackless country with the hardships incident thereto so imperiled Austin's health that he reached home an invalid, and died early the following June.

The Spanish authorities at Monterey, after granting Austin's petition on January 17th, sent Don Erasmo Seguin to the United States to communicate to Austin the result of his petition, and to officially conduct Austin and his three hundred families into Texas. Moses Austin received the information that this petition had been accepted while on his death bed and passed to his son, Stephen F. Austin, the legacy of fulfilling the commission.

THE LAST OF THE VICEROYS

The act of the Spanish Commandant at Monterey in accepting Moses Austin's petition and according him the privilege of colonizing three hundred American families in Texas, was the first and last of its kind ever made by the Spanish authorities of Mexico or New Spain. It was a complete reversion of the Spanish policy of more than two centuries. Very recently Texas historical students have found an old decree of the Spanish Cortes passed in 1820 authorizing the Spanish authorities in Mexico to grant colonization privileges. This decree does not seem to have ever been published either in Mexico or Texas, but evidently instructions with reference thereto had been sent to the Spanish authorities in Mexico, and this may account for the granting of Austin's petition. But this grant to Austin of January 17, 1821, was among the last acts of Spanish sovereignty in Mexico. The war for Mexican independence had been raging for more than ten years.

Augustin de Iturbide was a Spanish officer of great ability and lead the royalist forces. He had been called the Prince Rupert of the Spanish Army. On February 24th, 1821, he suddenly changed allegiance and announced himself in favor of the patriot cause. On that date he published the celebrated Plan of Iguala, which is regarded as the official beginning of Mexican independence. From that time on it was obvious that the Spanish authority in North America was practically at an end. In August, 1821, Don Juan O'Donoju, the 62nd, and last of the Spanish viceroys (and he was an Irishman), arrived at Vera Cruz to assume the government of Mexico. He at once saw the futility of further effort to maintain Spanish sovereignty, and set about to arrange a peace in which there would be some advantage to Spain, and sought a compact by which some member of the Spanish royal family would become ruler of Mexico.

On August 23rd, 1821, Santa Anna arranged a meeting between the new Viceroy and Iturbide, and on September 23rd, mounted on a black charger, Iturbide entered the City of Mexico amidst a scene of wild enthusiasm. He was tendered golden keys upon a silver platter by the first Alcalde of the city, and Mexico in point of fact became on that date an independent nation and began that long, pitiful career of anarchy which with slight intermission has prevailed for a hundred years. On the 7th of October, 1821, O'Donoju (O'Donohoo), scholar, gentleman and diplomat, broken in health and spirit by the loss of New Spain to his country, died in the City of Mexico and was interred in the Chapel of Los Reyes. Bancroft observes that with the celebration of his funeral rites the last shadow of vice regal presence and power passed forever.

While these events were going forward in Mexico, Stephen F. Austin, the first of the empresarios, was pushing the enterprise begun by his father, and he did not learn of the change of sovereignty that was taking place until he reached San Antonio in August, 1821. He went to New Orleans early in the year and began preparations for carrying out his great plans. Upon hearing that the petition had been granted he left New Orleans in June, 1821, and went up to Natchitoches to meet Seguin, who came there as the special envoy of the Spanish government to convey official notice of the grant of January 17th to Moses Austin.

STEPHEN FULLER AUSTIN, THE FIRST & GREATEST EMPRESARIO

Stephen F. Austin can easily be recognized as one of the great colonial leaders of the English-speaking people.

When we reflect that it was less than fifteen years from the advent of his first colony in December, 1821, until the Battle of San Jacinto and the Republic, one must look in vain for so great an achievement in so short a time elsewhere on this continent.

The Spanish Commandant at Monterey had dispatched Don Erasmo Seguin to the States to inform Austin that his petition had been granted, and Don Erasmo, with a small party of Spaniards from San Antonio, had proceeded along the Old Spanish Trail to Natchitoches, Louisiana, where they waited to meet Moses Austin. Austin's failing health had warned him of his approaching death, and he arranged for his son, Stephen, to come from New Orleans and meet Seguin and take charge of the enterprise. Stephen left New Orleans on June 18th, 1821, and proceeded to Natchitoches, where he met Seguin and received formal confirmation of the Spanish grant to his father.

On July 2nd, 1821, Austin and his small party, along with Seguin's party, left Natchitoches for San Antonio by way of Nacogdoches. Austin was accompanied by a few daring spirits who, hearing of his proposed plans, had joined him on his first journey to Texas. Among those who rode with him were Doctor James Hewetson, well known in the early colonial days. A few years later Doctor Hewetson joined with James Power in founding the Power and Hewetson Colony of Irish immigrants in southwest Texas. The last glimpse we get of Doctor Hewetson was in 1842, when he was practicing medicine at Saltillo and administered mercies to the unhappy men of Mier.

William Little, from St. Louis, accompanied Austin. He afterwards located his headright league in Fort Bend County, where he lived for many years, and his plantation became a steamboat landing in the later days of Brazos Navigation. On July 10th, as the party proceeded towards the Texas frontier, a message overtook them bringing to Austin the melancholy news of the death of his father, which had occurred in Missouri on June 10th. The party pressed forward and on Monday, July 16th, 1821, entered the province of Texas and rode on to Nacogdoches, which they reached on July 20th. In Austin's report of their visit to Nacogdoches he says: "This place was in ruins. There yet remained one church, seven residences, and a total population of thirty-six inhabitants." The whole of this thirty-six were assembled and received instructions from Don Erasmo representing his Catholic Majesty, the King of Spain. He advised the people of Nacogdoches that it was the King's pleasure that the whole community move further east toward the Louisiana line, and they one and all acquiesced in this modest request, and agreed to migrate eastward upon short notice. Don Erasmo advised that he would return from San Antonio in the early autumn and complete the details for this exodus. These matters of state having been properly dispatched, the whole party proceeded on towards San Antonio, which was the next habitation.

SAN ANTONIO–ONE HUNDRED YEARS AGO

From Nacogdoches to San Antonio is not so far in these Pullman days, but it was quite a journey one hundred years ago.

Austin and Seguin, along with their little party, left Nacogdoches on July 21st, following the old San Antonio Road. They supplied themselves with meat by killing deer and buffalo as they went along.

On Sunday, August 12th, they reached the Guadalupe, where they went into camp, and a messenger from San Antonio met them there bringing news of the independence of Mexico. There were fifteen or twenty Spaniards in the party, and they received this information with manifestations of great joy.

The party arrived at San Antonio three weeks after leaving Nacogdoches and considered that the journey had been made in a very reasonable time.

Old San Antonio, the most interesting city in Texas, is rich with rare traditions dear to the student of history. It had its beginnings more than one hundred years before the advent of the Austins, and had been the most important place in Texas during the last century. The chain of missions, now in ruins, which one yet sees along the river, are evidence of futile efforts of Spain to evangelize and colonize north of the Rio Grande. Authorities vary as to the population of San Antonio at this time, but from the best information obtainable the population varied about as much as the reports that we now get. It was a floating and more or less transient populace and varied from 3,000 to 5,000. A few years before, Colonel Zebulon M. Pike, of the United States Army, had come through Texas charged with a mission from President Jefferson, and he gives a very interesting account of his short visit in San Antonio, where he reports having met some very refined and cultured Spanish people. For the most part the inhabitants dwelt in miserable houses with mud walls and grass thatched roofs. During the more than two centuries which had preceded, the Spanish title to Texas had been in much doubt and the policy of rigid exclusion which had prevailed was due to the fear that either French or English explorers would traverse the country and lay claim to it. Spain was very much in the position of a man who claims a tract of land with a doubtful title and who is depending upon its possession alone to supply the defects in his title.

When it was evident that the Spanish missions would fail, the whole colonization scheme seems to have been abandoned.

In 1730, nearly one hundred years before the time about which we write, the Spanish government made an effort to transplant people from its island colonies to Texas and actually brought fifteen families from the Canary Islands who were permanently located in San Antonio. This plan was not carried further because of the great cost of transplanting these people. The feeble and futile efforts of Spain to reclaim and colonize the vast territory are shown in remarkable contrast when we contemplate that it was just fourteen years from the time that Stephen Austin first rode into San Antonio in August, 1821, until he lead the patriot army of 1835 which drove the Mexicans out of that city. Austin and his American colonists did far more for Texas in the first few years than had been accomplished by Spain and the Spaniards during more than three centuries. Austin remained in San Antonio from August 12th to the 21st, in conference with the local authorities.

Martinez, who had been governor in December when Moses Austin was in San Antonio, was still governor in August when Stephen reached there. While it was generally recognized that Mexico had become independent, yet the actual transfer of authority did not occur until Iturbide made his entrance into the City of Mexico in September following.

AUSTIN IN SAN ANTONIO

While in San Antonio from August 12th to 21st, 1821, Austin and Governor Martinez reached a general understanding as to such details as seemed required under the original grant made by the Spanish authorities at Monterey in the preceding January. In the letter of acceptance which Martinez had written Moses Austin in February, 1821, he referred to the fact that some of the immigrants might come by sea, and called attention to a port which the Spanish government had recently opened on the Bay of San Benardo, and he advised Austin that this port be used as a place of entry. While Stephen Austin was in San Antonio, Governor Martinez gave him a formal letter under date of August 14, 1821, giving him meager instructions as to the country he might explore, and asking that when he had explored it and decided upon his exact location, that he, Austin, report to the Governor. In this letter Martinez says:

You can proceed to the River Colorado and examine the land on its margins which may be suited for the location of your Louisiana families, informing me of the place which you select in order that when they arrive a competent commissioner may be sent out to distribute the lands, and inasmuch as they may come by sea, they must be landed in the Bay of San Benardo, where a port has been opened by the Superior Government.

The letter continues, giving Austin authority to take soundings of the Colorado River to its mouth. The inference is that this port was at the mouth of the Colorado, and the San Benardo Bay referred to in these letters must have meant Matagorda Bay.

Martinez requested Austin to furnish a plan for the distribution of land to the new settlers. Austin proposed one which would give the head of each family and each single man over age 640 acres, 320 acres in addition for the wife, should there be one, 160 acres in addition for each child, 80 acres in addition for each slave. This plan was presented in writing, and Austin received authority from the Governor to promise that guaranty to his settlers. This plan was afterwards materially changed but is interesting as the first plan accepted and the one first advertised by Austin in the United States.

There is much that is interesting and romantic when one contemplates Austin as he left San Antonio August 21, 1821, and went out into a vast and, to him, unknown country to seek and locate his empire. The facilities for travel were so meager, the guides so ignorant and the trails so indistinct, that it was indeed a plunge into a wilderness.

If one will take the map of Texas and study for a moment the large area between San Antonio and the coast and thence to the north and east toward the Sabine, he will get a glimpse of the great land which lay before the ambitious young adventurer as he rode out of Bexar on that August day one hundred years ago. It is the great Gulf hinterland traversed by the San Antonio, Guadalupe, Colorado, Brazos and various rivers which flow down to the sea through one of the fairest countries in all of the world. Unlike all the latter colonial grants, there were no fixed boundaries to the first one and Austin was left with few restrictions to select his own territory in which to locate the first three hundred. The nearest definite destination which Austin seems to have had when he left San Antonio was the mysterious port on the Bay, San Benardo.

AUSTIN EXPLORES THE GULF LITTORAL

The Spanish Governor, Baron de Bastrop, Don Erasmo Seguin and other local dignitaries bade Austin a formal goodbye with many protestations of Castillian friendship as he left San Antonio on the morning of August 21, 1821, following the road to Goliad.

In those days there still remained a fragment of the La Bahia mission settlement which had been undertaken in the last century. An indistinct Spanish trail reached from the Gulf through La Bahia on toward Natchitoches, Louisiana. It had been used by traders and smugglers for more than one hundred years. At La Bahia Austin divided his company, sending all surplus horses and mules on to Natchitoches, after which he explored the coast country. He reached the headwaters of Matagorda Bay on September 6, 1821, and continued skirting the coast toward the Colorado. On September 10, he passed the site of La Salle's settlement, where 135 years before the French had made a sad effort to locate a colony. There is indeed an interesting picture, when one contemplates the young American standing at the ruins of the old fort which told of the failure of the bold and brilliant La Salle. It was a wild, desolate spot one hundred years ago, and the nearest human habitation was the squalid little settlement at Goliad which he had passed a week before. The Frenchman's dreams were to discover and claim the vast realm west of the Mississippi for his King. He gave his young life in this hopeless quest and sleeps in an unknown grave somewhere in South Texas. Austin, though less romantic than the French cavalier, had hopes as high and ambitions as vast as those which lured La Salle, and had the far better fortune to live long enough to see his dreams realized.

After passing the grave of the French enterprise, Austin rode on to the Colorado to seek the port of entry which had been so warmly pressed upon him by the Spanish Governor. He reached the Colorado on September 15, 1821, and explored it down to the Bay, and having also explored the lower Brazos he felt that he had found his land of promise and hurried back to Natchitoches in order to complete arrangements for leading his colony into the wilderness. Few men in our history have a higher claim to greatness than Stephen F. Austin both from the standpoint of character and merit as well as material achievement.

A latter day writer who has summed up his career and understood his hardships, has said of him, "He carried out his father's enterprise with a patience that amounted to genius and fortitude which was the equivalent of the favor of Heaven."

AUSTIN'S RETURN TO THE STATES

Austin reached Natchitoches on his return from his first trip to Texas, October 3, 1821, three months to a day from the time that he and Seguin with their company had left that place for Bexar. He felt that everything was permanently arranged for his advent into Texas with his three hundred. There had been considerable notoriety given to his proposed colony during the summer of 1821; while he was yet in Texas. Louisiana and Mississippi papers widely published the reports which he gave out upon his return to Louisiana in October, and the spirit of adventure which was rife in those days turned wide attention to the new country, which during the farthest recollection of men then living had been closed to all the world save the Spaniard and the wild Indian. Fairy stories of the great land west of the Sabine had been told throughout the States for many years. It was known that its prairies teemed with millions of wild horses. It was known that cattle and buffalo abounded there, and little was needed to arouse universal interest in a land so vast that no man knew its boundaries.

Moses Austin's plan to colonize Texas was not a spasmodic impulse. It is known that he had cherished such an ambition for years, though what fed his hopes of ever getting Spanish permission is difficult to say at this remote date.

After the Spanish treaty in 1819, in which Florida was ceded to the United States and that country had recognized Spanish sovereignty in Texas, Moses Austin felt that all objection to American colonization should be removed and he planned applying to the Spanish government at Madrid for this permission. He was told, however, he should make his application to the authorities in New Spain, and this occasioned his first journey to San Antonio in December, 1820. Like most men who nourish a great enterprise, Moses Austin had faith in its success and faith in himself. He began to plan for taking his colony into Texas even before he first applied himself to the Spanish authorities for permission. He believed his application would be granted, and early in 1820 he had sent Stephen Austin with equipment and men necessary to open a large plantation on Red River just across from Texas in Arkansas at a place called Long's Prairie. He planned to establish a kind of gateway here through which immigrants would pass and to furnish supplies and facilities for forwarding people who would apply for entrance into Texas. As early as June in 1821, there were families in Arkansas and Missouri waiting the word from Austin to move into Texas, and in that month, while Stephen Austin was yet on his way to Bexar, several families left Pecan Point, Arkansas, for somewhere in Texas, and reached the Brazos in what is now Washington County, in December, 1821. Upon Stephen Austin's return to Louisiana in October, 1821, he addressed himself with his usual industry to organize expeditions to move into Texas by land and by sea. While the first contingent of Arkansas and Missouri immigrants were coming across the country through a trackless wild, a vessel with people and supplies was sent out from New Orleans in November, 1821, bound for the Texas Coast.

THE NEW YEARS CREEK COLONY

While the first overland immigrants were plodding their way into Texas in the autumn of 1821, the schooner *Lively*, which Austin had fitted out in New Orleans, made its way to the Texas coast. There is a mystery about the *Lively* which one hundred years has not cleared up, but there is no uncertainty as to the identity of the little advance guard which reached the La Bahia crossing on the Brazos late in December, 1821, camped on what they called New Years Creek in what is now Washington County, January 1, 1822.

Austin had left New Orleans after arranging for the voyage of the *Lively*, and hurried up to Natchitoches, from whence he had joined these overland immigrants and was with them when they lighted their New Year's campfires in the wilderness which was to be their homes and the homes of their children for the centuries to come.

When Austin and his wagon train halted here at the La Bahia crossing, they found two American families who had preceded them just a few days. These first arrivals were Garrett and Higgins, but more than this we have no detail as to who they were or whence they came. Many years later, Guy M. Bryan (1852) gave the name of Andy Robinson, then living in Brazoria County, as the first settler in Austin's Colony in Washington County. The names of the first three hundred who constituted Austin's Colony are well known and are preserved both in Austin's records and in the records of the land office. If there are descendants of this New Years Colony yet living who can from family tradition give any detail as to the first year of this colony, they would supply information much needed in Texas history. Such descendants, wherever they are, are entitled to all of the glory that comes from a splendid heritage—as much entitled to that distinction as the descendants of those who came on the *Mayflower*.

The people of Texas should ever feel a deep interest and perpetual pride in the memory of those simple pioneer folk who laid the cornerstone of the commonwealth on New Years Creek one hundred years ago. Within a few weeks James B. Austin, Stephen's brother, and Josiah H. Bell of South Carolina joined this settlement. In after years Bell and his honored family became well known in Texas. He located his headright grant of two leagues of land on the west bank of the Brazos River, in Brazoria County, and the great Columbia oil field is largely on his grant. Bell's landing was an important place in the navigation of the Brazos River for many years. Judge James H. Bell, son of Josiah, was born in the colony and was a member of the Supreme Court of Texas at the outbreak of the war between the states.

As soon as the first details were arranged and the New Years Creek colonists had begun hewing their houses, the tireless Austin hurried down the river to meet those who had come by sea on the *Lively*.

THE SCHOONER *LIVELY*

The first expedition of Austin's colonists by sea left New Orleans on the ill-fated schooner *Lively*.

Joseph Hawkins, who had been a college mate with Austin and who was a prosperous Southern lawyer, enthused over Austin's Texas plans, financed this expedition. Austin and Hawkins stood on the dock at New Orleans and saw the little boat, freighted with its immigrant passengers and a miscellaneous cargo, sail for Texas on the morning of November 22, 1821. The next day Austin left New Orleans by boat for Natchitoches to join the overland party with which he came on to the Brazos.

The *Lively* carried seed for planting, various implements of husbandry and eighteen immigrants, several of whom had been with Austin on his journey into Texas in the preceding summer. The boat had instructions to go to the mouth of the Colorado and into the mythical port of entry which had been so highly recommended by Governor Martinez in his official correspondence with the Austins. After many days floundering about in the Gulf, the vessel unloaded its cargo and most of its passengers at the mouth of the Brazos in December, 1821, some days before the New Years Creek Colony pitched camp 150 miles up the river. As the *Lively* came through Galveston Bay, it encountered a pirate ship which ran away, and saw the ruins of a schooner which had been scuttled and beached on the island. Piracy on the high seas flourished in those days and had been a rather romantic pastime for gentlemen of adventure since the Spanish ships had first begun bringing home Mexican gold three hundred years before. This manly art, however, was in its last stages, and the exodus of Lafitte from Galveston Island under pressure from the United States government only a few years before marked the beginning of the end of robbery on these seas.

When the captain in charge of the *Lively* unloaded at the Brazos, he went further west to find the Spanish port in the Bay of San Bernardo and to await the coming of Austin, who was to meet the vessel there. The available data leaves much doubt as to the course and career of he *Lively* after it left the little company of immigrants at the mouth of the Brazos and spread sail for the west. Some say it found entrance to the Colorado River and reported a fine harbor. Others that it never found the river. Others say that it returned to New Orleans and brought out a second cargo early the next year and was wrecked on the end of Galveston Island. (This is the most likely version.) There are others who say that the captain sailed away with the boat to some Mexican port and sold it and spent his thirty pieces of silver in riotous living. And there was even a rumor among the pioneer folks that it turned pirate and roved up and down the Spanish Main.

The immigrants left at the mouth of the Brazos River made their way up the stream on foot and in a small row boat, and after weary weeks reached a place where the prairie to the west came down to the river's edge, and located themselves and began a first settlement upon the spot which is now the town of Richmond on the Brazos. Richmond may well lay claim to the honor of being the first settlement in Austin's Colony, and the first Anglo American town in Texas. Before they left the mouth of the river, they were joined by one William Morton and members of his family, who had come in a small boat from Mobile. His boat had been wrecked, and he and those with him were thrown ashore to begin life with the *Lively* immigrants. In going up the river the immigrants were on constant lookout for Austin's overland colonists, whom they expected to come down the river. William Morton remained at the site of this first settlement, and at a later date located his headright grant of two leagues on the east side of the Brazos River across from Richmond. The Southern Pacific bridge across the river spans the stream at a point where Morton's leagues touch its margin. In the meantime Austin left his New Year's Colony and went across to the Colorado and down the river to meet the *Lively* at the "Spanish port in the Bay of San Bernardo." He remained in this vicinity for nearly three months waiting and watching for the ship that never came. It was a long, tedious wait in an inclement winter, but this tenacious, patient man never wearied in his watch as long as there was any hope that the vessel would come.

The cargo that it carried seemed indispensable to his first colony and its loss seemed insuperable. After these weary weeks of waiting, he mourned the loss of his entire merchant marine and hastened on to San Antonio to report progress to Governor Martinez. He went up the Colorado River to where the Bahia Road crossed the stream and there met a party including his brother, J. E. B. Austin, and Josiah Bell and others, and they proceeded on to San Antonio. He had been almost continuously in the saddle for more than a year and the trails and hardships that he had endured, including the loss of the *Lively*, were indeed severe, but all these things were meager when compared with the trials and tribulations that awaited him in the immediate years to come.

AUSTIN GOES TO MEXICO

Austin reached San Antonio the second time on the 22nd of March, 1822, and reported immediately to Governor Martinez. It had dawned upon the governor in the interim since Austin went away in the preceding August, that the change of sovereignty in Mexico might affect his authority, and it had also been suggested to him that he had gone too far in agreeing with Austin upon the quantity of land Austin could promise his settlers. In any event this worthy Spanish gentleman was reticent and more or less disturbed when Austin called to see him, and advised Austin that he go to the City of Mexico forthwith and take up the further details with the new Mexican government. Iturbide had been acknowledged as the executive head of the government since he entered the City of Mexico in the preceding September, and had called a Congress which was about to meet, and it was to this new authority that Austin was directed to apply himself. He did not speak the Spanish language. He had not come prepared for such a journey, his presence seemed indispensable to his colonists, but with his characteristic promptness, he left immediately for the City of Mexico, leaving Josiah H. Bell in charge during his absence.

A journey from San Antonio to the City of Mexico in those days was one of hardship and peril. It was a distance of 1200 miles through a wild country infested with Indians and brigands of all kinds. He rode out of San Antonio accompanied by Doctor Andrews, who went with him a portion of the way. On the second day out they were surrounded by Comanche Indians, but Austin knew enough of the Indian language to make his peace with them. They got away, however, with some of his chattel effects, among them a Spanish grammar that he carried on his saddle so that he could study the Spanish language as he went along. Just what the Comanches wanted with this Spanish grammar is not clear, but at any rate it was found in the possession of a roving band of Indians north of the Red River several months later. Austin's name and address were written in it, and the rumor got back to his home in Missouri and to his relatives there that he had been murdered by the Comanches.

After crossing the Rio Grande, he was advised it was not safe to proceed without an armed guard, but he and his companion, Christie, left Monterey on foot disguised as beggars. They improvised a story that they were poor patriots who had served in the revolution that had lately succeeded, and that they were making a pilgrimage to the capital to ask the new government to remunerate them for their services. On the 29th of April, 1822, after thirty-six days spent on the way, Austin the first time saw the City of Mexico. He found the capitol in a turbulent, noisy mood, for Iturbide was concluding his arrangements to assume the title of Emperor.

The Plan of Iguala under which Iturbide had operated since the preceding February, tendered the Mexican throne to Ferdinand VII, then the Bourbon King of Spain, conditioned, however, that he would remove to Mexico and bind himself to support a constitution to be promulgated by the Mexican people. Ferdinand declined the honor under the onerous conditions named, and it occurred to Iturbide that it would not be well to let the proffered crown go by default, so he contrived with much shrewdness to have himself proclaimed Emperor. Austin was present in the city and saw this done on the 18th day of May, 1822, when Iturbide annexed the euphonious title of Constitutional Emperor of the Mexican Nation and Grand Master of the Imperial Order of Guadalupe.

The first Mexican Congress had assembled at the call of Iturbide in the previous February, and was in session when these things occurred, and though the Congress was summoned by him and supposed to be composed largely of his creatures, it did not approve of his imperial designs, and immediately after he assumed or usurped this high authority, there began a many-cornered fight between the Emperor and the Congress and various other factions which has proceeded with remarkable regularity even unto this day.

In the midst of these scenes of national chaos, Austin, a perfect stranger in a wild, weary land, without money and without friends, and bereft of his Spanish grammar, entered the City of Mexico seeking the proper authority to confirm his grant.

And back on the Brazos fifteen hundred miles away, the advance guard of the Old Three Hundred, as his first colonists were called, fought hardships unspeakable as they waited his return.

The season was unfavorable and the venison lean that year in the colony, and Austin's persistent patience at the Mexican capital was no greater than that of his people whom he had left behind.

THE EMPEROR ITURBIDE

When Austin first reached Mexico in the last days of April, 1822, the first Mexican Congress was in session, and the supreme authority was supposed to be vested in a *junta* or committee with Iturbide at its head. Within a very few days after his arrival, he saw the junta, or the regency, as it has sometimes been called, converted into the Empire. Iturbide, who had himself declared Emperor in May, 1822, assumed the title of Augustin I, and many other high sounding titles. The empire over which he figuratively ruled was the third in territorial extent of all the nations of the earth. It reached from Yucatan in the tropics to the far north along the Pacific, probably to Oregon, and its eastern and northern borders between it and the United States included with Texas nearly seven of our present western states.

The first Congress continued in session for some months after the empire was proclaimed, and at the urgent instance of Austin and other persons from the United States who were there seeking similar concessions, a colonization committee was appointed for the purpose of framing a suitable colonization law. At that time no active opposition to permitting colonization in Texas seemed to have manifested itself, although it is now known that many prominent Mexican leaders doubted the wisdom of this plan from the beginning, and in a very few years they succeeded in bringing about legislation which was designed to stop further immigration from the north. The publication in the papers of the United States of Austin's first concession in the summer of 1821, caused a number of more or less prominent and adventurous Americans to flock to the City of Mexico for the purpose of getting similar concessions, and the presence and activity of these persons materially embarrassed Austin in his plans. Austin immediately filed a memorial with the colonization committee giving the history of his and his father's activities, and pointing out that he had gone so far as to bring his first colonists into Texas, and urging immediate ratification of the grant made to his father on January 17, 1821. This concession would probably have been promptly ratified but for the presence of these other persons seeking similar concessions, and on this account it was thought best that the Congress pass a colonization law governing all such grants, and in the usual tedious, tardy way that such things have from time immemorial been handled in all countries, the matter dragged itself along through the entire summer. There were many committee meetings and proposed drafts and redrafts of a colonization scheme. Austin was present at many of these meetings, and had made such progress in learning the Spanish language during the first few months, despite the loss of his Spanish grammar en route, that he was enabled to materially assist the committee in drafting the first colonization law. In fact there is a pretty fiction that during this time he made a tentative draft of a constitution of the Republic of Mexico which was used as a model in the formation of the Mexican constitution of 1824. This may, or may not be, a pure fiction, but it is well known that he assisted in forming the first colonization law, and that he got the first and only national colonization grant.

The first Mexican Congress, however, was a very unstable institution. It seemed to sit more or less during good behavior, and the pleasure of the emperor, and though Austin sought to hasten his matters, haste was not an attribute of the first Congress and especially of the colonization committee of that Congress. His first efforts were directed toward a special act confirming his grant for the reasons set forth in his memorial. But failing in this, he succeeded in having matters so advanced that the committee all but finished a colonization law in October, 1822. Austin's frankness and persistent patience had won him not only the respect of the congressional committee but the warm friendship of some of the more substantial Mexican leaders, including Hererra and Andres Quintana. The proposed colonial enactment was completed all but the last few sections in the latter part of October, 1822, and it was promised passage through Congress within a few days. Austin now saw what he deemed the end of his labors in Mexico, and after six months of weary waiting, expected to take his way homeward within a week. But the storm which had been brewing between the Emperor and the first Congress burst in all its fury in the latter days of October, and on the last day of the month, an officer from the Emperor's Army entered the congressional chamber and read a message from his Imperial Highness, Augustin I, dissolving the first Congress sine die and giving the members thereof ten minutes, Mexican time, in which to disperse. And within this incredulously short time it did disperse. In parliamentary language, his decree of dismissal or dispersal had the emergency clause attached. This incident is without parallel in Mexican history. The only thing the Mexican people have ever since been known to do in ten minutes was to start a revolution. With the going of the Congress went the colonial committee, and went also the first draft of the proposed national colonization law, finished all but the last three articles.

Poor Austin was left to begin all over again and doomed to other long weary months of work and waiting. And back on the Brazos there was a deep malarial gloom.

THE END OF THE EMPIRE

The reign of Iturbide was short, but while it lasted he was an Emperor of the old school. He dissolved the first Congress on the last day of October, 1822, attaching the emergency clause to his decree of dissolution giving the members ten minutes to vacate and with positive instructions to remain vacated.

The American colony in the city which had been lobbying for the passage of a colonization law, with the hope of getting colonization contracts, were much discouraged, and some of them left the city and abandoned the enterprise. When the Emperor had dissolved the Congress, he determined that Mexico should be ruled by himself with the assistance of a junta, the members of which he would appoint, and he proceeded to name this committee or junta, called in Mexican literature, the Junta Instituyente, and this high sounding institution, composed of the Emperor's select men, proceeded to administer the affairs of Mexico for a few brief weeks.

Austin made haste to address himself to the Junta Instituyente, to whom he presented his memorial and urged his suit. He went over again the long story that he had told the congressional committee. The Emperor's Junta Instituyente was less unwieldy than the Congress, and through the influence of Herrera and Quintana and others whose friendship Austin had made, his petition had a favorable hearing, and the matter proceeded with unusual dispatch for Mexican affairs. The draft which had been all but completed at the time of the dissolution of the ten minute Congress, was resuscitated and the last three articles added, and on January 14, 1823, almost two years from the date his father had received the first grant (January 17, 1821), Austin received a favorable report from the committee recommending the historic colonization law of 1823. But the committee could not pass the law, only the Emperor could give it final sanction, and it went to His Majesty with a favorable recommendation.

On February 18, 1823, Augustin, by divine providence Emperor of Mexico, etc., etc., formulated his decree permitting the law to become effective *insofar as a grant to Austin was concerned but no further*. In view of the special merit and the equitable reasons that surrounded Austin's case, his grant or concession was ratified, but the Emperor's decree did not put the law into general effect or permit other colonial grants.

Now at last it seemed that Austin's hopes were realized, and again he was ready to start to the north, but before he could get out of the city, the fall of Iturbide's government was manifest.

Santa Anna, Bravo and others had begun a revolution against the Empire which was thundering away in many parts of Mexico. On the 19th of February, the very next day after Austin got his decree, Herrera, his friend and counselor, and who stood high in the Emperor's government, fled from the city in the night and joined the revolution. Before Austin could get away, the storm broke in all its fury and on the 21st of February, 1823, Augustin, Emperor of Mexico and Grand Master of the Imperial Order of Guadalupe, who had a few short months before entered the city in a blaze of glory, mounted upon a black charger, and had received from the first Alcalde a golden key upon a silver platter, marched out the Puebla Road never to return.

Austin's Grant Confirmed

The fall of the empire left Austin in much uncertainty as to the status of the colonization law and of his grant. The Junta Instituyente had passed it on the 14th of January and the Emperor had approved it in so far as Austin's concession was concerned on February 18, but no man knew what the status of any of the legislative or executive acts of the late government would be upon the incoming of the new regime. There was nothing that Austin could do but watch and wait. Still more of the members of the American colony who were there urging their claims for grants became discouraged and went away.

In March, the National Congress met, the same which on the last day of the previous October had been dissolved by the Emperor under the ten minute order. One of the first acts of the new session was to nullify everything that had been done during the enforced recess of the Congress. A triumvirate was named and vested with supreme power. Austin lost no time in presenting himself again to the new Congress. He had now become almost a perpetual petitioner. Governments had risen and fallen so rapidly during his stay in the city that one could scarcely keep account of the swift changes, but he found some of his old friends in the new session, with whom he had labored on the colonial committee at the previous session. In course of time the law which had been passed by the Emperor's Junta Instituyente was resurrected and the new congressional committee determined to approve it far enough to authorize Austin's concession, and then suspend it as to all other applicants until further notice. Both Congress and the new executive triumvirate approved the concession to Austin that had been made by the late Emperor in the preceding February, their approval being given April 14, 1823. The concession to Austin thus finally approved by the national government was the first, last and only national grant ever made to lands in Texas. After this concession was approved it was the policy of the national government to place upon the Mexican states the responsibility of colonial legislation, and under the system subsequently adopted all future grants were made by the legislature of the State of Coahuila and Texas. Thus for the fourth time in two years Austin had seen the ever-changing governments approve his concession, and he hurried out of Mexico, and remembering the fate of Lot's wife, did not dare look back for fear that he would see another revolution on the horizon, and indeed he did live to see many more, though his career was brief. Many strange and adventurous characters had foregathered in the Mexican capital in those days, lured by the hope of getting grants similar to that made to the Austins.

When Stephen first reached the city in April, 1822, he found a group of this gentry, some of whom remained during the entire time that he was there. Among them were Haden Edwards, a prodigal Kentuckian who afterwards made history and trouble in and about Nacogdoches; Green DeWitt, who in later years founded DeWitt's Colony on the Guadalupe; General James Wilkinson, who at one time had been Commander-in-Chief of the Armies of the United States, and whose name has always been more or less mixed with Aaron Burr in his supposed conspiracy. But the most pathetic of all the supplicants who gathered there was a committee of Cherokee chiefs who came from East Texas to urge their claims upon the new government, and to beg a home for their wandering people. The Cherokees were a relatively docile and semi-civilized people, who at one time had occupied a vast region from Virginia to Georgia, but who had been driven west of the Mississippi. These poor people had come to know that a man must have some kind of a paper title in order to hold land, and they conceived the idea that if they could get a grant from the Mexican government that they might hold their hunting grounds in the land where they had located north of the old San Antonio Road and east of the Trinity. There is yet in existence a pitiful letter written by Richard Fields, chief of the Cherokees, voicing their woes. It is interesting, yet pathetic, when we reflect that it comes from a people lately and rightfully Lords of the continent. It is so unique that this generation might well read it, the last wail of a now vanished race:

Feburey the fust Day 1822 Apacation mad to Subsprem Governer of Provunce of Spain.

Dieor Sur: I wish to fall at your feet and omblay ask you what must be Dun with us pur Indians. We have som Grants that was give us when we live under the Spanish Govt and we wish you to send us news by next mal whether the will be reberst or not and if wer committed we will com as soon as posble to persent ourselves befor you in a manner agreeable to our talants, etc.

Richard Fields
A Chaf of Charkee Nation

But the chief of the Cherokees, Edwards, DeWitt and the various other applicants who presented their claims at Mexico during these troubled times, were made to await the colonization law passed the next year, 1824, and only Austin, out of all the petitioners, was permitted to enter.

THE TERMS OF THE FIRST GRANT

A study of the first Mexican colonization law finally passed by Iturbide's Junta in 1823, though subsequently suspended, is one of the most interesting chapters in Texas history. It never actually became operative, but it formed the groundwork of subsequent legislation covering land grants during the whole colonial period. Many of the terms and expressions found in the act of 1823 have come down to us as household words.

Governor Martinez had no instructions from any superior authority giving detail as to the lands Austin could offer his colonists. In fact this subject never seemed to have been considered in the earlier correspondence or at any time prior to Stephen Austin's first visit to San Antonio in August, 1821. Martinez at that time asked Austin to outline a plan for distribution of land, and he proposed for each single man or head of a family, a section one mile square, or 640 acres, and 320 acres additional for the wife, 160 additional for each child, and 80 for each slave. Martinez acquiesced in this proposal, and Austin seems to have had no doubt as to its authenticity, and advertised it extensively, and this was the bounty which the first colonists expected. When Martinez reported these things to the Superior Commandant at the City of Mexico the question was at once raised as to his authority to make this arrangement, and the Governor urged Austin to go on to Mexico and straighten the matter out when the latter reached San Antonio the second time in March, 1822.

All of the various governments and departments of governments with whom Austin dealt during the more than one year he remained in the City of Mexico on his first visit declined to ratify Martinez's agreement as to the quantity of land, though they were all willing to recognize the merits of Austin's claim, and anxious to facilitate him in carrying out his colonial scheme. This promised to embarrass Austin very much, as his word had gone out to his colonists, and his plan had been widely advertised in the United States. He urged and explained these things to the colonial committee of the first Congress, and yet it was obdurate in refusing to accede to his wishes. The colonial committee named the *labor*, which was a survey 1,000 varas square and containing 177 acres, as the unit of quantity. This quantity was the amount to be assigned to each person who proposed to engage in agriculture. It was explained to the committee that this would be inadequate for those who proposed to engage in stock raising as well, and some ingenious person made a motion that the act be so drafted as to permit a larger quantity to be given to those who proposed to become herdsmen and engage in the ancient avocation of stock raising. This suggestion found favor, and the act was so drawn that while a person who would engage in farming *alone* should be

given a labor and no more, yet if the colonist also contemplated stock raising he should have in addition to his
labor a *sitio* or a league of land, as we have come to call
it. It may be remarked in passing that Austin's colonists
seem to have been stock raisers and took the league along
with the labor. They developed a wonderful predilection
for this pastoral profession. There is much humor in this
situation. Austin urged the colonial committee to ratify
a plan under which he had offered 640 acres of land to
each head of family, and a possible additional quantity of
several hundred acres which in no event could amount to
more than half a league, and though the committee stub-
bornly refused to authorize such an arrangement, it nevertheless provided for a plan by which each colonist could
(and practically all of them did) get a league and labor.
He asked for a section and they gave him a league. In fact
the act was so drawn that if the colonist proposed to raise
much stock, he could have more than a league, and in
many instances two leagues and even larger grants were
made. The John Austin survey, upon which a very large
portion of the City of Houston is located, is a two league
grant, and William Morton, whose headright lay on the
Brazos opposite the City of Richmond, had a two league
grant. There were many such in the colony.

There were many other interesting provisions in the
law of 1823, not the least of which was one regulating
slavery which provided, "after the publication of this law,
there can be no sale or purchase of the slaves which may
be introduced into the Empire, and the children of slaves
born in the Empire shall be free at fourteen years of age."

This act of 1823 is the one which was finished all but
three sections on the last day of October, 1822, when the
Emperor dissolved Congress under his emergency order.
It was completed and adopted by Iturbide's Junta in January, 1823, and sanctioned by him in February. The Congress which assembled on the fall of the empire in March
thereafter first revoked this law by general order, then

recognized it for the purpose of confirming the grant to Austin, then suspended it after ratifying Austin's concession under it with the notation, "that hereafter said colonization law passed by the Junta Instituyente shall be suspended until a new resolution on the subject."

This new resolution on the subject was a national colonization law passed in 1824. It will be seen, therefore, that the law of 1823, with its unusual stormy career at birth, all but passed in October, adopted in January following, ratified by the Emperor in February, set aside by the ten minute Congress in March, reaffirmed by the same Congress in April, in order to authorize Austin's grant, suspended by the same Congress immediately after Austin's concession was adopted, and thereafterwards postponed, though it never became a law, nevertheless constituted the framework of subsequent Mexican legislation, and its provisions had a material bearing upon all of the Texas colonies.

AUSTIN'S GREAT ACHIEVEMENT

One cannot follow the course of events narrated in these articles without developing the greatest admiration for Austin and the highest respect for his character and genius.

He went to Mexico in April, 1822, without money, without acquaintances, unable to speak the language, and even robbed of his Spanish grammar, and at a turbulent time when no man's mind was normal. He found the city full of adventurers using influence and intrigue to get colonial concessions in Texas. Without any of these blandishments, he alone succeeded. Every department of every government which he approached during the many changes of the eventful year when he was there, heard him with approval and ultimately granted his concession. At the time he reached the City of Mexico, he was only twenty-eight years old. He had left school at seventeen, and when scarcely twenty-one had been elected a member of the Legislature of Missouri Territory, in which body he had served for six years.

In 1820 he was appointed Federal Judge in Arkansas, and in 1821 was about to engage in a newspaper venture in New Orleans, when called to take up his father's enterprise. There was nothing in his education and training which fitted him for the unusual mission upon which he went to the City of Mexico. When he rode north in April, 1823, with his grant finally approved, he was not yet thirty, but all other suitors who had not abandoned the quest remained behind to await later legislation. No greater tribute to Austin's genius can be paid than by the simple recital of these historical facts. Since the grant which the government made to him alone and affected his first colony only, and since it differed materially from those of later date made both to him and other empresarios, it is of peculiar interest.

Governor Martinez, in August, 1821, sent Austin away into the Gulf Coast country with a wave of the hand to find a location for his first colony along the Colorado River. There was much discussion between Austin and the authorities in Mexico while he was there in 1822-23 as to what should be the boundaries of his first colony. It was finally settled in the Emperor's decree of the 18th of February, and later approved by the Congress as follows:

> With respect to the demarkation of limits for the new establishment described by Austin in his memorial, the council are of the opinion that it need not be granted because there is not sufficient data to ascertain the extent of the territory and because the Colony will be composed of the land granted in full property to the colonists.

In other words, the lands granted to the individual settlers wherever they might locate would constitute the extent of the first colonial grant. Three hundred and seven separate colonial land grants were made under this decree, and they were scattered over the wide area now known as the following counties: Fayette, Burleson, Austin, Washington, Waller, Grimes, Harris, Chambers, Fort Bend, Brazoria, Matagorda, Wharton, Colorado and Brazos. The outside limits of this territory are as wide as the boundaries of the state of Massachusetts, and show the aversion that our ancestors had against being crowded. The only limitation imposed was a restriction against any grant within the "littoral border" or within ten leagues of the Gulf Coast. None of the grants of the first colony were within this zone. It was reserved from settlement for the time being with the idea that the government should control the coastline. This policy was relaxed a few years later, and Austin's fourth colony covered the entire Gulf littoral from the Lavaca to the San Jacinto. It is evident now when looking back upon events which transpired one hundred years ago, that but for two things there would have been no colonial grant prior to the national law of 1824, and possibly not then. There is even a possibility that there would have been no national law authorizing colonization but for the influences which brought about the first concession. These two things were: First, the character and personality of Austin and the great impression he made upon all the official bodies with which he came in contact during his year's stay in the capital.

Second, there was a spirit of fairness involved which these governments were willing to recognize. The Spanish sovereignty had made a concession to Austin and his father which he spent a year in fulfilling. It was far performed on his part and his reputation and fortune were wrecked if it were not carried out. The Mexican officials manifested a spirit of fairness and equity toward Austin in these matters which is indeed commendable. The other would-be empresarios who haunted the ante-chambers of these Mexican governments did not inspire so much confidence, nor did they have any claims upon the government as Austin did. There was even in those days a current of grave suspicion among many Mexican leaders against the wisdom of allowing colonists from the United States to settle in Texas, and looking back upon the situation now one is lead to wonder at the great stupidity of the Mexican governments in ever permitting this movement. In less than six years from this very time Mexican leaders boldly spoke out against it and would have undone all that had been done, if it were possible. Had it not been for the ever-recurrent revolutions which followed each other in Mexico during these years, it is more than likely that the first colony would have been wiped out long before it reached a point where it could maintain itself.

It was manifest to those Mexican leaders who gave the subject much thought that these American colonists could never become Mexicans, either in sentiment, politics or religion, and these thoughts may well have turned the scale against colonization entirely but for the great interest and confidence that Austin inspired and the masterful way in which he urged the justice of a ratification of his first concession. His name and influence and character gave a coloring as it were to the whole colonial scheme, and in the wake of his coming the other empresarios crept in. And now, after the lapse of one hundred years, it is not too much to say that the hand of Stephen F. Austin, raised at this time and under the circumstances here detailed, determined the fate of all the country north of the Rio Grande, and that Texas and the western states were to be Saxon rather than Latin. This is not merely fulsome praise. It is rather a tardy acknowledgment of the real merit and great work of this remarkable man.

Surely very few men in American history have wrought so much, and his achievements and their effect upon our history class him as a national figure—a national hero.

THE FIRST COLONISTS

The first colonial grant to Austin, of February 18, 1823, afterwards confirmed by the ten-minute congress on April 14, 1823, directed him to collaborate with the governor of Texas or a commissioner appointed by the governor, to designate and divide the land among the colonists. Austin was authorized to locate a town at a place central to the colonists, which should serve as the seat of government for the colony. Above all, the colonists must be Roman Catholics of steady habits. This was supposed to be indispensable. He was authorized to organize the colonists into a militia, and until the government was further organized, he was charged with the administration of justice, a settlement of all differences which might arise among the inhabitants, and the preservation of good order and tranquility. It must be remembered that this first grant, with its broad powers conferred upon Austin, was made before the Mexican Constitution of 1824, and more than three years before there was a constitutional state government for Coahuila and Texas.

Austin stopped at Monterey on his return, for a conference with the state authorities, and was designated as a Lieutenant Colonel, and was afterwards known as Colonel Austin, until he was elected commander-in-chief of the colonial forces at Gonzales, in 1835, after which he was called General Austin.

The Governor of Coahuila and Texas, Don Luciano Garcia, appointed that genial soldier of fortune the Baron de Bastrop Commissioner to issue the titles to the colonists, and in 1823, Austin and Bastrop arrived in the colony. This same Don Luciano issued a letter of instructions to Bastrop on July 23rd, asking him to locate and lay out the town called to be established in the colonial concession, and named San Felipe de Austin.

During the year which lapsed since the first colonists arrived, and while Austin was in Mexico, some progress had been made toward permanent settlements. Emigrants had come singly and in companies, by land and by sea, and had squatted at various places, from La Grange to the mouth of the San Jacinto. There is a poetic interest when one reflects upon the prospect which confronted these ancestors of ours, as they wearily wended their way into a vast, strange, virgin land and selected sites for their homes, as convenience, or fancy, or accident suggested. One family would be attracted by a beautiful grove, another by a charming landscape. All of them kept an eye singled to fertile lands and gravitated to the alluvial river fronts. One hardy Tennessean, who had come overland nearly a thousand miles, stopped on the Brazos early in 1822, and was about to make his permanent location. After a few days, he heard that a fellow from Alabama had located five miles below him, and in disgust at such unseemly crowding, he folded his tent and moved across to the Colorado.

The details of surveying and locating the lands and issuing the titles called for a vast amount of work. The names of Samuel M. Williams and Horatio Chrisman should ever be remembered in connection with the location of the first colony. Williams came from Maryland, in 1822, and in his application for a land grant it is recited that he spoke both the Spanish and French languages, as well as the English. [He was made Secretary of Austin's Colony and labored with Austin throughout all the colonial period. The volumes of land records made during these years were all in Williams' handwriting. Chrisman and Ingram and the other surveyors who made the first locations would write their field notes as the work progressed, in English. These field notes were often written on odd scraps of paper. But before the grant could issue, the field notes had to be translated into Spanish and all of the official records, including the grants themselves, were in the Spanish. Williams, however, preserved the original field notes, and they have been bound into a volume, which has been kept even unto this day.

The first survey in the colony is said to have been the one made for Josiah H. Bell, on the west side of the Brazos, a few miles below the La Bahia Road. This work was done on the tenth of February, 1823, by Horatio Chrisman. Ingram's first survey was made for Sylvanus Castleman, on the west side of the Colorado above La Grange.

The first year in the colony was a very hard one, and this eight-cylindered generation can never know the hardships and privations which these people suffered during the first years. Many families were without bread until the first corn crop was matured. The talented Horatio Chrisman were a leather hunting jacket all summer because he had no shirt. The family of William Morton lived largely on lettuce for months. But the mustang ponies were fat and more easily killed than deer and meat was reasonably abundant.

GOVERNMENT OF THE FIRST COLONY

While Austin was yet in Mexico in 1822, the first colonists having settled on the Colorado and Brazos Rivers, Governor Trespalacios, who had succeeded the Spanish governor, Martinez, took authority to divide the new colony into two districts, that of the Colorado and of the Brazos, and named an Alcalde for each district. This was the first political recognition of the new colony, and James Cummings, provisional alcalde of Colorado, appointed by Don Felix Trespalacios, in 1822, was the first Anglo-American civil officer ever named in Texas.

When Austin and Bastrop returned to the state in 1823, a letter had preceded them from Saucedo at Bexar, advising the alcaldes of the appointment of Bastrop. The letter to Alcalde Cummings is printed among Austin's papers and directs him to assemble his people at the house of Sylvanus Castleman, On the Colorado, to hear instructions regarding the grant to Austin and Austin's authority. The alcalde is a petty Spanish judicial officer. The office is one of great antiquity and the alcalde is supposed to be as indispensable to a Spanish community as a justice of the peace is found in an English neighborhood.

Austin accepted the alcalde arrangements made for him in advance, and set about the location of his capital and the promulgation of a civil and criminal code, which were published in 1824. These codes, entirely written by him, remained the law of the colonies, until the first ayuntemientos were established in 1828 and constitutional alcaldes chosen. His criminal code consisted of twenty-six articles, and is dated January 22, 1824. The five first articles are devoted to the proper handling of Indians, and provide that if Indians are found in a neighborhood and their conduct leads to the suspicion that they intend to steal, they should be apprehended and taken before the nearest alcalde, who is given power to punish them if he deems it necessary. Article five concludes the treatise on Indians, in this unique language:

"No person in the colony shall ill treat or abuse any Indian without just cause, under a penalty of one hundred dollars, but shall treat them at all times in a friendly manner, so long as they deserve it."

After thus disposing of the Indian question, the law-giver proceeds in article six to fix the status of other criminals, making it the duty of all persons to apprehend them before an alcalde. If the criminal makes a resistance, it is lawful to kill him. Gambling of every description is prohibited under a heavy fine, but horse racing, "being calculated to improve the breed of horses," is not classified as gambling.

In article nine he made it a high misdemeanor for a man and woman to live together without being married, but suspended this section until sixty days after the arrival of the first priest, who was expected to take up his residence in the colony in due time.

Five sections of the penal code were devoted to offences

concerning slaves and slavery and by slaves, and it was made a heavy offence to steal a slave. The code named the crimes of theft, assault, slander, counterfeiting, and provided for a jury trial in the Alcalde's Court. All fines collected were to go to the benefit of a school fund and other public purposes.

This miniature code, promulgated by Austin in January, 1824, was the law of the land for more than four years, and is interesting as the first English code ever written in Texas.

In his civil code, Austin provided for a constable in each district, to serve the process of the alcaldes. Here was a rare blending of the English and Latin forms of jurisprudence. Think of an English constable serving the process of a Spanish alcalde. The civil code provides for the form of the alcalde's docket, and there are yet in existence a number of these old dockets, which bear some very interesting recitals. I have examined the old alcalde registers of Brazoria, which bear the names of the attorneys who practiced in those remote days, and frequently among them appear such names as John A. Wharton, R. J. Townes, Elisha M. Pease, and others afterwards well known in the early history of Texas.

The twenty-third section of the civil code provides that in case no property of a debtor can be found by the Constable, that his body should be seized and the alcalde should examine into his circumstances, and in case it should be found that he had fraudulently conveyed away or concealed his property, then the Alcalde may hire out the defendant to the highest bidder, until his wages pay the debt.

During these four years, Austin's life was an extremely busy one. In a sketch recently written by Eugene Barker, the following glimpse is given of his unusual activities:

It would be impossible to exaggerate Austin's labors in the early years of the colony. A letter to the political chief, in 1826, gives a clue to their character and variety. He had left San Felipe on April fourth, to point out some land recently conceded to one of the state officials, and had been detained by excessive rains and swollen streams, until the twenty-ninth. On May first, he began the trial of an important case, that lasted seven days. At the same time, he had to entertain a delegation of Tonkaway Indians and make preparations for a campaign against another tribe; to talk to and answer questions of many foreigners who had come to look at the country, explaining and translating the Federal Constitution and laws for them; to receive and pass upon applications for land, hear reports and issue instructions to surveyors; and to correspond with superior civil and military officers at San Antonio and Monterey. Much of his time was consumed in settling neighborhood disputes about cows and calves. During these years, he gathered, by painstaking surveys and personal observation, data for a map of Texas, published by Tanner, in 1829, charted Galveston Bay and the harbors and navigable rivers of the state, promoted trade with the United States, and kept a stream of immigrants flowing into the colony; encouraged the erection of gins and sawmills and the establishment of schools; exercised throughout a most remarkable influence over the legislature at Saltillo, in matters affecting the interests of the colonists.

In addition to the affairs of his own colony, he was called upon in every critical situation that arose in the other colonies, and especially DeWitt's and Edwards' colonies. His high standing with the Mexican officials and the great deference they paid to him gave him an influence that was sought, not only by his own colonists, but all other empresarios. He established the seat of government for his colony at a site located on the Brazos River, now in Austin County. A tentative location was first made on the Colorado, but this was abandoned for San Felipe, and a five-league grant of land was made by the Mexican government, on which to locate the town. San Felipe remained the seat of government until the advance of Santa Anna's army in 1836.

EMPRESARIO GRANTS

Austin's first grant was finally approved on the fourteenth day of April, 1823, but the same act which approved it provided that no other grant should be made until the passage of a state colonization law for Coahuila and Texas, and that all subsequent grants should emanate from the state government. The other empresarios (or contractors) were therefore compelled to await the organization of the state government. These would-be empresarios who foregathered at Mexico in 1821 migrated to Saltillo, the little capital of Coahuila, and in March, 1825, when the first state statute was passed authorizing such grants, there was no dearth of applicants at Saltillo. On the fifteenth day of April, 1825, the first state grants were made. On that day, Green DeWitt received the contract to locate four hundred families between the Guadalupe and the Lavaca; Robert Leftwitch, four hundred families north of the San Antonio Road and between the Brazos and the Colorado; Frost Thorne, four hundred families in East Texas; and on the eighteenth, Hayden Edwards, who had been waiting and watching four years for such a concession, had permission to locate four hundred families in East Texas, in the neighborhood of Nacogdoches. On the twenty-seventh of the same month, Austin received a concession for his second colony, which gave him permission to locate three hundred families, within the bounds already occupied by his scattered first colonists.

Many other grants were made during this and succeeding years, so that between 1825, when the Land Office was opened at Saltillo, and 1835, when it was closed by the Revolution, there had been thirty-two grants, covering almost the entire territory now embraced by the state of Texas. The great majority of them were never fulfilled. Austin afterwards received two other colonial grants, his third colony covering the territory between the Brazos and the San Jacinto. During the first few years, no grants were made within the Gulf littoral, which included a strip ten leagues in width, from the mouth of the Rio Grande to the Sabine. When Austin came to locate his fourth colony, however, he got permission to locate it entirely within this Gulf littoral and it extended from the mouth of the Lavaca to the mouth of the San Jacinto. Of all the other empresario grants that were made during these years, only those to Austin were entirely fulfilled. DeWitt's was probably more nearly fulfilled than any of the others.

Martin DeLeon, a Mexican, procured permission in 1825 to locate a colony, and did locate it, founding the city of Victoria, which was settled at first by Mexican colonists. McMullen and McGloin procured a grant, between the Nueces and San Antonio Rivers, south of the San Antonio Road, and located an Irish colony there. Some of these grants were early forfeited and relocations made. Many of them were made the basis of wild land speculation in the United States.

Three large contiguous grants, covering practically all of Southeast Texas east of the San Jacinto River, were made to Burnet, Vehlein and De Zavala. The land covered by these grants extended from Galveston Bay along the Sabine River to the Nacogdoches Road, and Burnet's grant lay north of that road. The three grants embraced 1,000 leagues, a territory almost as vast as one of the Southern states. These gentlemen conveyed their holdings to trustees, among whom were William H. Sumner, of Boston, United States senator from Massachusetts; and a company was formed, known as the Galveston Bay and Texas Land Company, which took the title of the empresarios to the property, and stock was issued and offered for sale. They procured the opinion of no less an authority than Chancellor Kent as to the validity of these grants, and their plan of operation, and started on a scheme of rather wild land speculation. Austin protested very bitterly against these things. It created a bad impression in Mexico. He had started out to bring in bona fide colonists, people who would settle and develop the country. This land speculation, which began as early as 1826, is often given as one of the causes of the Revolution.

THE HAYDEN EDWARDS GRANT

Edwards was in Mexico, seeking a grant, when Austin went there in 1821. Yoakum says of him that he kept open house and entertained very lavishly. It appears from Austin's correspondence some years later that Edwards operated a roulette wheel in this open house, which probably increased the lavishness of his entertainments. Edwards was an impetuous, quick tempered person, the very kind of a man that would not be calculated to get along well with Spaniards or Mexicans. He made his headquarters at Nacogdoches, where he found a very small settlement at the time of his coming. Nacogdoches had been a substantial settlement years before, but had been destroyed in 1818, and when Austin came there in 1821, the town did not contain but half a dozen houses and thirty or forty inhabitants. The news of the opening of Texas to American emigrants, however, caused a great influx of people into all East Texas, and Nacogdoches soon became a relatively important place.

During 1825 and 1826, there was a gathering of renegade Mexicans in East Texas and about Nacogdoches—refugees who had left Mexico for its good—and the same class of gentry from the States soon foregathered there and formed a congenial society for evil. Edwards and his emigrants soon came into conflict with this element, and as is usually the case, there was a harmony between the bad elements, both American and Mexican, which came into direct antagonism with Edwards and his well-meaning colonists. Nacogdoches was the only place in Texas, except San Antonio, where there was any Mexican population worth mentioning, and of course the only place where there could be any friction between the inhabitants and the newcomers. That such friction was inevitable must have been apparent to everyone, and that it manifested itself at the very beginning is but natural.

A Mexican rogue named Sepulveda, more or less skilled in forgeries in general and in land forgeries in particular, and an American rogue named Norris, skilled in many forms of villainy, conspired together so that Norris was chosen alcalde of the new settlement.

Edwards, with a frankness, and in good English, informed Governor Blanco at San Antonio of the deeds and misdeeds of Sepuleveda and his gang. Governor Blanco thought a bad Mexican was much better than a good American, and on this score sided with the renegades and canceled Edwards' empresario grant and expelled him from the colony. Colonists were coming in great numbers to locate under Edwards' concession and he had spent almost a fortune in the enterprise, and this turn of affairs meant his ruin. He and his brother, Benjamin, determined to defy Blanco's authority, and on December 16, 1826, Benjamin Edwards rode into Nacogdoches and declared the existence of the Republic of Fredonia, and unfurled its flag, in the grim wake of a Texas norther, which howled in the East Texas pines that night.

In desperation for an ally in this emergency, the Edwards turned to the Cherokee Indians, who dwelt in the woods north of the San Antonio-Nacogdoches Road, and an offensive and defensive alliance was formed, by which the Fredonians and the Cherokees were to work their independence and then divide East Texas equally.

There was a rather celebrated globetrotter named John Dunn Hunter, whose journeys and voyages through the world had been more thrilling, if possible, than those of Sinbad the Sailor. At this particular time, he was in some way connected with the Mexican government, as an agent among the Cherokees. Hunter and Richard Fields, the Cherokee chief, manipulated this new alliance with the Fredonians.

Austin had foreseen this trouble and as early as March of this year, 1826, he had written Edwards a long, scathing letter, frankly telling him that his course of dealing and his indiscreet utterances would get him into serious trouble. After reviewing various rumors as to Edwards' doings and sayings, the young empresario warned the old man thus: "One moment's reflection will show you the imprudence and impropriety of such utterances as those attributed to you." Edwards and those associated with him, foreseeing this crisis, had sent letters to many influential men in Austin's Colony, urging them to join in resistance to the Mexican authority, and most of these letters had been forwarded to Austin, or called to his attention. Austin knew the utter folly of Edwards' course, and foresaw that if any suspicion attached to him or his colonists, that the whole colonial scheme would be wiped out. He therefore used every endeavor, not only to suppress the rebellion, but to show the Mexican authorities that he was in accord with them, and that he had no sympathy with the Fredonian movement.

THE FREDONIAN REBELLION

When news of the arrival of Edwards, with his Fredonian army of fifteen persons, was carried to the authorities in Mexico, there was a great hurrying to and fro, and military preparations to suppress the rebellion were begun on a large scale. It was confidently believed by the people of Mexico, and by many of the Mexican leaders, that this was the first effort of the United States of the North, as they called our country, to claim Texas, and they confidently believed that they would be at war with the United States, as soon as their forces reached Texas.

The Mexican Congress voted a large sum of money to defray the expenses of the campaign and an expedition of troops was arranged to be sent by Vera Cruz, to land in Galveston Bay and march overland to Nacogdoches. Arrangements were put on foot to send an army across the Rio Grande. Long before these ambitious plans were underway, however, the rebellion had collapsed with its own weight and under the pressure of the local military authorities.

Colonel Ellis P. Bean, who had come into Texas with Nolan in 1812, and who had spent several of the intervening years in a Mexican dungeon, and had in this way become a naturalized Mexican citizen, resided near Nacogdoches in those days. The story of Bean is an interesting and romantic one, but I will not stop to relate it here. He carried the title of Colonel of Militia under the Mexican government, and had authority to look after matters pertaining to the Indians. Being an American, he was mistrusted by the Mexican authorities, and being a Mexican official, he was mistrusted by the American colonists. But Colonel Bean assumed authority to take action against the Fredonian rebels and moved on to Nacogdoches.

Saucedo, the Mexican political chief at Bexar, sent a detachment of two hundred men by way of San Felipe. From San Felipe, and after a conference with Austin, Saucedo issued a mighty manifesto to the colonists, reviewing the entire Nacogdoches trouble and advising that on the morrow, January 22nd, 1827, he would march on to Nacogdoches. Austin felt that the fate of his colony was at stake and that if there was the least suspicion of his loyalty, or his sympathy with Edwards, that all was lost. There were no more than a thousand American families in all Texas at that time, and the destruction of the entire colonial venture would have been an easy matter. Then, too, Austin was under the deepest obligations to the Mexican government. Whatever the treatment of Edwards might have been, yet the authorities at Mexico had been fair to Austin, and held him in high esteem. In order to give public evidence of his position in the matter, he raised a detachment of men from his colony, to accompany Saucedo's army. In addition to this, Austin sent a committee to Nacogdoches, composed of Richard Ellis, James Cummings and James Kerr, with instructions to investigate and report, and to use their influence to induce the revolutionists to forbear. Austin's committee made an interesting report, advising that they had met Edwards and John Dunn Hunter, and that they were unwilling to accept amnesty, but would insist upon absolute freedom of all the country north of the Rio Grande.

On January 4th, before Saucedo's men, along with the colonial troops, could reach Nacogdoches, Alcalde Norris had raised an army of sixty-seven loyal men, and with this force, marched into Nacogdoches to give battle to the Fredonian forces. The Fredonian army had disbanded for the day, not expecting any hostile activity, and when Alcalde Norris' army appeared, only eleven white men and nine Indians were available for defense. They rallied, however, and defeated the government forces, this being the only active engagement that was fought. One Fredonian was wounded and one of Norris' men killed.

In the meantime Colonel Bean had started a counter intrigue with the Cherokees. Austin and Saucedo wrote letters to Fields and Hunter, but these leaders were bent on revolution. Through Bean's influences, however, dissension was brought about among the Cherokees and they held a council of war and decided to rescind their late agreements with the Fredonians and ally themselves with the Mexican authorities, and as evidence of their good faith in this new alliance, they ruthlessly slew Dick Fields, the Cherokee chief, and John Dunn Hunter, the celebrated globetrotter.

After some skirmishing, and shorn of their Indian allies, the Fredonians fled, and the Mexican flag again floated at Nacogdoches. The revolution was at an end before Saucedo's army arrived, and that doughty warrior was denied the pleasure of military triumphs.

Edwards and the Fredonians, and their premature, ill-starred revolution were gone, but like the song of John Brown of Ossowatomie, their souls went marching on. Men of more judgment and discretion wrought what they so wildly aimed at.

THE EFFECT OF THE FREDONIAN REBELLION

The rise and fall of Fredonia, though apparently a small matter, of local significance only, was in fact far otherwise. It was the first skirmish in the trouble which ended at San Jacinto, to be renewed again in the Mexican War with the United States, twenty years later. Its importance was not overlooked at the time, either in the United States or Mexico. There were wild rumors all through Mexico that it was an instigation of the government of the United States, with designs to claim the Rio Grande as a boundary.

So strong was this feeling in Mexico that in 1827 Henry Clay, Secretary of State in the cabinet of John Quincy Adams, addressed a letter to Obregon, the minister from Mexico to the United States at that time, expressing regret at the occurrence and disavowing any sympathy with it. Mexico was so profoundly stirred that great preparations were made to invade Texas by land and by sea, for the purpose of putting down the Fredonians and warring with the people of the United States, whom they confidently believed would come into the fray. One thousand men were marshaled to come by sea, and ten thousand were designed to march overland. When the news of the fall of the Fredonians was received in Mexico, this contemplated army of invasion turned its attention to an internal revolution which was brewing. The strange aspect of the Mexican colonial policy, which invited and admitted people from the United States to settle in Texas, becomes stranger still when we fully understand the eternal feeling of suspicion and mistrust which existed toward the United States in Mexico during these years, and one must candidly admit that subsequent events seemed to justify this suspicion. Those were the days when the Democratic party, committed to the domination of the slave-holding element in the South, was in the ascendancy, and designed to rule the fortunes of this country and shape its policies, until the outbreak of the Civil War, in the next generation.

The eternal quarrel as to the boundary line between the Spanish and French possessions in America, or between Louisiana, which was nominally considered French, and Texas, which was considered Spanish, had lasted for two centuries, and when the United States acquired Louisiana from Napoleon, it succeeded to this boundary line dispute. There was much reason for France to have contended that Louisiana extended to the Rio Grande. In fact, the French title, based on the explorations of La Salle, was about as good as any title which Spain could assert. The United States, as successor to the French title, could have insisted upon the Rio Grande as the boundary between Louisiana and the Spanish possessions in Mexico, but prior to 1820, the American people were more interested in the navigation of the Mississippi River and in possession of Florida and the elimination of all Spanish claims in that quarter than in the remote western boundary of Louisiana. This accounts for the De Onis Treaty, of 1819, concluded during the first administration of Monroe, by the terms of which Spain ceded all claim to Florida and the United States recognized the Sabine and the Red River as the southwestern boundary of Louisiana. Within two years after this treaty was ratified, Mexico achieved its independence, and the question arose as to whether it was bound by the treaty or could insist upon its recognition by the United States. Just how there could be any question about it, I cannot see, but nevertheless it seems to have been much debated and it was currently believed in Mexico that the United States would make the contention that the treaty was not binding upon it as against the new Mexican nation, that country not having been a party to it. Then, too, there was a general feeling in the United States that in some way the treaty would either be abrogated, or ignored and set aside, and the United States would acquire Texas.

The very first minister from Mexico to the United States, in 1822, discovered this feeling and hastened to warn his government of it and to exaggerate it into a widespread conspiracy to occupy all the country north of the Rio Grande. As early as October, 1822, Zazaya, first Mexican minister, wrote his government, after he had been in the United States only a few weeks, that he had discovered ambitious designs with reference to Texas, and this letter and similar warnings were in the hands of the Mexican officials when Iturbide and his committee, as well at the Ten-Minute Congress, approved Austin's first grant, in April, 1823. In that year, Torrens, who had become Mexican minister at Washington, continued his warnings, and in August, 1823, sent specific recommendations against allowing the American population to become predominant in Texas. These reports were so frequent and so alarming as to cause the Mexican government to take urgent steps to have the De Onis Treaty so recognized as to make it binding on the United States and to work out the boundaries with great precision.

On April 15, 1824, the political chief at San Antonio wrote to the government at Mexico: "The American government counts Texas its own and even included it on its maps, tracing its boundaries to the Rio Grande." Yet on this very day, April 15, 1824, the authorities at Saltillo granted Green DeWitt, Hayden Edwards and Frost

Thorne vast colonial tracts, covering large portions of Texas. The fears of Mexico in this behalf were fanned into white heat by the Fredonian outbreak, and after it subsided, they were continuously kept aroused by repeated efforts of the United States to purchase Texas. From the beginning of the John Quincy Adams administration, in 1824, until the Revolution, in 1836, the State Department at Washington never ceased its efforts to induce the various governments, which abode their destined hour in Mexico, to sell Texas. Joel Poinsett, our minister to Mexico during the Adams administration, was instructed to buy Texas, and Henry Clay, Secretary of State under Adams, wrote him volumes upon the subject. He was told to make an effort to get the Rio Grande as a boundary, failing in that to try for the Lavaca or the Nueces of the Colorado, or even the Brazos, and was given a scale of prices for these various boundaries; but every offer made to every one of the rapidly changing governments in Mexico was met by a flat refusal. At one time, Poinsett wrote Clay, in 1825, that if the United States would let up on its efforts for a few years, the American settlers then pouring into Texas would become so boisterous and troublesome that Mexico might be more willing to sell Texas, to get rid of them. In one of Clay's letters to Poinsett, he suggested that it be called to Mexico's attention that the United States was better equipped to take care of the Comanche Indians than Mexico, and that if it acquired Texas, it would take it over, Indians and all, and would look after these troublesome people.

With the incoming of the Jackson administration, in 1828, these activities were renewed or accelerated. Jackson sent one Anthony Butler, of infamous memory, as minister to Mexico, and he began a six-year course of treacherous intrigue which became the scandal of the day, all designed to beg, bribe or steal Texas away from the Mexican Federation. Mexican leaders during these years became almost hysterical about the designs of the

United States, and they had much indeed upon which to found their hysteria; but all of the time, new grants were being made to empresarios and the stream of colonists continued unabated, until 1830. Mexican papers from time to time published attacks on this government, and in the Mexican Congress it was openly charged that the United States and its people were natural and deadly enemies to Mexico. These contradictory things are hard to understand a hundred years after.

GENERAL MANUEL MIER Y TERAN

There is an interesting and pathetic glimpse of the times, 1828 to 1832, found in the biography of this brilliant and gifted man. General Teran had been a leader in the patriot cause during the war for independence, 1810 to 1821, and followed the varying fortunes of the rebel army during these long, bitter years. He was a man of great intellect, splendidly educated and of sterling character. The earlier Texas historians have contented themselves with rude flings at Teran, and indeed he was not a prime favorite with the Texas colonists, but at this date we can look back upon his character and career and realize in him a really great and patriotic man, who tried to serve his country with as much fairness to the Texas colonists as seemed consistent with his own country's safety.

When the boundary question with the United States became acute, the Mexican Congress passed numerous resolutions and acts and imposed treaties designed to adjust it, and a commission was created, to go upon the ground and mark the boundary with proper monuments. In 1827, shortly after the Fredonian incident, General Teran was sent to Texas on this commission. The purpose of his mission, however, was much broader than the mere locating and marking of the Texas boundaries. Among the specific instructions that he is known to have received from the Minister of Relations in the Mexican cabinet, was to make a report upon the desirability of maintaining garrisons and troops at various points in Texas. He journeyed to Bexar and after a visit there, stopped for a time at San Felipe and visited other points in Austin's Colony. Here he formed an acquaintance and intimate friendship with Austin, who seems to have won Teran's confidence and admiration. From San Felipe, he proceeded on to Nacogdoches, where he tarried for some time and studied the local situation.

General Teran wielded greater influence in Texas affairs than any other Mexican of his day, prior to Santa Anna, and his activities wrought much in our destiny. From the time of his visit to the date of his tragic death, in 1832, he was the eyes and ears and brains of Mexican officialdom in Texas. His reports to his government about Texas form a chapter of intense interest and can be better understood now, in the light of subsequent events. Every law and decree, as well as every movement or policy towards or affecting Texas during these years emanated from him, or from suggestions and recommendations that he made to his government. At the time of his arrival at Nacogdoches, a small garrison was located there, under the command of Colonel Piedras, who had been stationed there in June, 1827, after the Fredonian fiasco, to keep the peace and resist the aggressions of the United States of the north. Guadalupe Victoria was the first constitutional president of Mexico, and Teran was his intimate friend. From Nacogdoches, Teran made a lengthy confidential report to Victoria, which is a very interesting and important document, showing a Mexican's insight into Texas affairs. One reading this letter sees in it seemingly strange contradictions, but they are the struggle of a strong man with a fate which he foresees, but will not admit.

In his communication he says that Mexican influence has about ceased in Texas, in fact that it is scarcely felt at all in East Texas, where the American population is both aggressive and thrifty, and the Mexicans poor and ignorant and the very lowest class. That the Americans maintain a school for their children, where they are taught in English, but there is no school for Mexican children. That it would cause his enlightened countrymen chagrin to see the contempt in which Mexicans are held by the foreigners, who have never seen or known any other Mexicans save these low, ignorant and thriftless fellows about Nacogdoches.

After recounting these things in great detail, he proceeds thus: "I tell myself that it could not be otherwise but that from such a state of affairs an antagonism will arise, which is not the least of the smoldering fires which I have discovered." He then points out the governmental difficulties of the colonists and states their grievances fully and fairly, and suggests the location of an appellate court at Nacogdoches. He is free in his expressions of admiration for the honest, industrious colonists, and points to their love of land ownership as a "strong virtue," but he foresaw the loss of Texas and made many suggestions to avert the disaster, which one can tell from his whole communication he knew was inevitable. The most urgent of his suggestions was the strengthening of the Mexican colonies in Texas.

During the next few years, Teran was Comandante General of the eastern provinces of Mexico, which included Texas, and he kept an eternal vigil on Texas and the Texans. In 1829, he wrote his government (a revolution had changed its personnel in the interim), giving his grave suspicions as to the intentions of the United States. In this letter, he suggests that the empresarios are instruments of the United States government, and he grows almost frantic, declaring he who consents to the loss of Texas is an execrable traitor, who ought to be punished with death. He hints that war may break out, and that if so, the colonists should be suppressed in a single campaign, and urges upon his home government plans to colonize Texas with Mexicans. He makes many other recommendations, all more or less visionary, yet in the face of all these facts, he did not recommend cessation of immigration, though he probably hinted at it. He would have immigration from the States restricted, though just what restrictions he would have were not clearly stated. He would not have Texas left an unpeopled wilderness, for then it would revert entirely to the Indians, and the United States might occupy it and claim it. He would not have it populated wholly by American colonists, for he feared they would turn it over to the United States. He seemed to want a limited immigration from the States, to act as a buffer against the Indians, and an immigration from Mexico so that Texas might have an increasing Mexican population.

And all the while that Teran visited, and wrote and planned, the stream of immigrants from the States continued.

GENERAL TERAN'S GARRISONS— MORE PEOPLE FROM THE STATES

General Teran's recommendations with reference to Texas found favor with the several governments which followed each other in quick succession in Mexico, for he was a friend of all the leaders until the ascension of Santa Anna in 1832. Teran found a strong ally in all of his activities and suspicions in Lucas Alaman, the ambitious young Minister of Relations under the Victoria government. Working in harmony with the administration, Teran hastened plans for establishing Mexican garrisons at various places in Texas, and Mexican convicts were impressed for this military service, and forces were stationed at Velasco, Anahuac, Nacogdoches and La Bahia. On April 6, 1830, the Mexican Congress, urged on by Teran and Alaman, passed the celebrated decree which forbade further emigration to Texas from the United States. It was the inevitable friction between the colonists and these military authorities which provoked the first trouble and which kept trouble going until the revolution in

1835-36. Garrisons of soldiers in charge of such men as Col. Piedras at Nacogdoches and the celebrated and infamous John Davis Bradburn at Anahuac, precipitated the strife which verified the worst fears of poor Teran. In the meantime, however, while Teran wrote frantic letters and Alaman wrought powerfully to save Texas,

American colonists continued to pour into the country by the thousands. There were estimated to be a thousand families here in 1826 when the Fredonian trouble arose; ten thousand people in 1828, and probably thirty thousand people in 1832. A great many strong and influential men came to Texas during the period from 1828 and 1832, men who became leaders during the succeeding years. Among those who came as early as 1828 were R. M. Williamson from Georgia, familiarly known as "Three-legged Willie," and as the "Patrick Henry of the Revolution;" Gail Borden, who came from New York; David G. Burnet from New Jersey; John A. and William H. Wharton from Tennessee, and many others whose names have become household terms in Texas. There was soon a widespread feeling among the colonists, and especially the new arrivals, in favor of a more positive policy, and following the advent of Teran's military garrisons there were many murmurings and much subdued talk of independence. The colonists continued to prosper, however, and the prosperity was in no small measure due to the slave-holding element, who were able to raise large crops of cotton for export.

After the organization of the Mexican government under the Constitution of 1824, Texas had remained a part of Coahuila, and whatever semblance of a state government it had depended upon the authorities at Saltillo and Monclova and such other Mexican places as were from time to time the capitals of Coahuila, a thousand miles away from the colonies.

Prior to 1828, Austin was the government of the colonies.

In 1827, a constitution was formed for Coahuila and Texas, and in the following year there was an organization of the state government under this constitution. The first election ever held in Texas was for members of the ayuntamiento of San Felipe in 1828. This council, when chosen, had jurisdiction between the Lavaca and San Jacinto Rivers and the sea. It composed all of Austin's Colony, and the new municipal body became the first authoritative local government, succeeding to many functions which had theretofore been exercised by Austin alone. Two hundred thirty-two votes were cast, and when the ballots were sent to Austin at San Felipe, it was found that Thomas M. Duke had been chosen Alcalde; Thomas Davis and Humphry Jackson, Regidores, and Rawson Alley, Sindico.

These officials with strange sounding names composed a local council with such functions as are necessary for local government. But in point of fact this council did very little, for the colonists required little government. There was no system of taxation, for the colonists were never required to pay a direct or ad valorem tax to the federal or state government, and the effort later to collect customs at the ports of Anahuac, Velasco and elsewhere on the coast met with such violent opposition that it was in effect abandoned after 1832.

BRADBURN AT ANAHUAC

One of Teran's garrisons was in charge of Col. John Davis Bradburn at Anahuac at the eastern end of Galveston Bay. This Bradburn was a renegade American, who began life as a small merchant, but his mercantile business languished somewhat and he was caught in an effort to steal some slaves from a Tennessee planter and incarcerated in the Columbia, Tennessee, jail. He escaped prison by the assistance of a saw which someone smuggled in to him, and found his way to Mexico, where he joined the revolution and gained some distinction as a patriot, and the favor of Iturbide, under whom he fought. At a later date he got a commission from the legislature of Coahuila giving him the monopoly of operating steamboats on the Rio Grande River, but his efforts at navigation prospered little better than his endeavors at slave stealing. In the meantime he had become a colonel in the Mexican Army, and we find him now in charge at Anahuac, where there was a considerable settlement of American colonists. Early in 1832 the population at Anahuac embraced a number of persons who afterwards became well known in the colonies, among them Monroe Edwards, William Barrett Travis, R. M. Williamson and Patrick C. Jack.

Bradburn, who was a low-flung fellow, soon began a series of intolerable tyrannies. He went up to Liberty, suspended the functions of the local ayuntamiento, and strolled up and down the coast country with a great show of military authority. Travis and Jack were heard to say something unkind about him, or something derogatory to his greatness, and he sent a squad of soldiers to arrest them and had them incarcerated, announcing that he intended to send them to Vera Cruz or some remote Mexican place to be court-martialed. This act of tyranny brought on what was probably the first political meeting or gathering designed to protest against Mexican tyranny ever held in Texas. There was a gathering at Brazoria, where it was decided that a committee should be sent to Anahuac to demand the release of Travis and Jack.

A committee composed of William H. Jack and Branch T. Archer went over to Anahuac and demanded a surrender of the prisoners. Negotiations for their release were unsuccessful and a small company was raised at Brazoria, for the purpose of going over and forcibly effecting their release. At that time there was a Mexican garrison stationed at Velasco at the mouth of the Brazos in charge of a Mexican colonel by the name of Ugartechea. The Brazoria committee waited on this military person and told him that they intended to go over to Anahuac and have a settlement with Bradburn, and requested that he remain quiescent and offer Bradburn no assistance during their absence. Among those who went from Brazoria were John Austin, Warren D. C. Hall, William H. Hall, William J. Russell, and others. On the way they were joined by Wiley Martin from Fort Bend, and F. W. Johnson and other persons from along the Brazos.

Bradburn heard of the approach of the colonists, and that they intended to affect the release of the prisoners, and dispatched a small company of cavalry to intercept them. The men from the Brazos, however, surprised and captured all of the cavalry and then proceeded to Anahuac, where they made an armistice with Bradburn which he hastened to violate. As they approached Anahuac, William J. Russell saw a Mexican sentry standing under a tree some hundred yards away and, by crawling in the grass, he got close enough to him to kill him at a single shot; and this was the first bloodshed in the long series of conflicts that ensued between Texas and Mexico. The men from the Brazos, however, were without artillery and fell back to Turtle Bayou, while they sent over to Brazoria for a small cannon.

While they were waiting at Turtle Bayou they had an opportunity to ponder over the situation. Here was a small handful of colonists about to bring on a conflict with a Mexican garrison which would bring down upon the people of Texas the entire Mexican nation. News had reached Texas about this time that Santa Anna had started a revolution in Mexico and that he had proclaimed himself the friend of the constitution of 1824, and while this little company awaited the return of the men sent for the artillery, the happy thought possessed R. M. Williamson that they should put in writing the causes for which they were contending, and he then and there presented to those with him for adoption the celebrated "Turtle Bayou

Resolutions." These resolutions set forth that the people of Texas were loyal to Mexico, that the taking up of arms was against the tyranny of Bradburn and other small military tyrants, and they declared against the Bustamente government and in favor of that great champion of the liberty of people, General Santa Anna. These resolutions served a very useful purpose, as we shall later see. In the meantime reinforcements arrived and the men from the Brazos moved on to Anahuac, captured the town and sent the Mexican soldiers back home and put Bradburn in the road to Louisiana, giving him a very limited time in which to reach the frontier.

THE BATTLE OF VELASCO

The men of Brazoria had put business before pleasure and had gone over to clean up Bradburn at Anahuac, before doing the same honor to Colonel Ugartechea and his command at Velasco, at the mouth of the Brazos. They exacted a gentlemen's agreement from the Colonel that he would "stay put" and would not send any reinforcements to Bradburn, or as it were, that he would be dormant while they captured Bradburn and ran his garrison out of the country. After this they planned to come back and do the same thing to Ugartechea, but it is not recorded that they told him in so many words that this was their plan, although he well may have surmised it. After they had gotten away and sent back for the cannon that was to be brought up, while the men of Brazoria waited at Turtle Bayou, Ugartechea repented of his inactivity and refused to allow boats carrying guns to Anahuac to pass out of the river. In addition to this, the Colonel showed some signs of activity about his fort, which indicated that he was putting himself in a high state of defense, and as soon as the business at Anahuac was done, these same Brazoria persons turned their attention to Ugartechea's garrison at Velasco. William J. Russell, who had shot the

Mexican sentinel at Anahuac, was one of the leading spirits in the Velasco campaign.

The volunteers who enlisted for the siege of Velasco selected John Austin captain. He was no kin to Stephen, but had come to Texas from New England at the beginning of the colonies. The fort was attacked by land and by sea. The navy was a small schooner which was temporarily anchored in the harbor, and which Admiral Russell impressed into the service for the occasion. They turned this simple little three-master into a man-of-war, placing two small cannon on its deck and eighteen riflemen mid-ships, who under the command of Admiral Russell, opened a bombardment from the river side of the fort. After the battle had raged for a night and a day, the fort surrendered. Seven Texans were killed and twenty-seven wounded. The Mexican losses were forty-two dead and more than seventy wounded. The terms of the surrender were, that Colonel Ugartechea and the small remnants of his forces able to migrate were to go back to Mexico. A few weeks later, Colonel Piedras of Nacogdoches, who commanded the only remaining garrison in Texas, was subjected to considerable trouble by the colonists in East Texas; and after some forty of his men had been killed, and as many wounded, he acceded to the suggestion that he go south, and moved out with the remnant of his garrison. With the passing of Piedras, the last of poor Teran's men were driven from Texas. This spontaneous uprising on the part of the colonists, and the bloody expulsion of the Mexican garrisons from Texas, would undoubtedly have brought disaster to the colonists, had it not been for the miraculous intervention of a timely revolution in Mexico.

Upon the fall of Iturbide, in 1823, the ten-minute Congress assumed authority, until the formation of the constitution in 1824, and Guadalupe Victoria, a great and good man, had been chosen first constitutional president. Near the close of his term, in 1828, a revolution resulted in Don Manuel Pedraza being named president; but he was not permitted to hold the office. Before he could get comfortably seated, another revolution, fomented by Santa Anna and headed by Guerrera, took the presidency *vi et armis.*

Bustamente was Guerrera's Vice President, and he promptly started a new revolution which in the following year raised him to the Presidency, and with the ascension of this boisterous usurper, Guerrera, one of the purest of all the Mexican patriots, was shot as a traitor.

It was during the term of Bustamente that the Decree of 1830 was promulgated, prohibiting the further immigration of people from the States into Texas. In 1832, Santa Anna, who had backed Guerrera against Pedraza, and who had secretly backed Bustamente against Guerrera, and who had consistently plotted against every government that had prevailed in Mexico since he was old enough to bear arms, started the annual revolution against Bustamente. News of Santa Anna's revolution reached Texas about the time the men of the Brazos were on their way to Anahuac. The people of Texas hoped and probably believed that Santa Anna was an improvement on those who had been President, and that he would keep his promise to maintain a constitutional government. At any rate, they declared for him and this was the excuse that they offered for the expulsion of the Mexican garrisons.

LONG LIVE SANTA ANNA

The four years which followed the expulsion of Teran's military men from Texas were the most interesting and important in all Texas history. Before entering upon an outline of things which happened between the exodus of Bradburn from Anahuac, in June, 1832, and the fall of Santa Anna at San Jacinto, in 1836, we can properly take an inventory as it were of the year 1832.

The news of the forcible expulsion of the Mexican soldiers from Texas made a terrific impression in Mexico. It was received there with the same apprehension that was felt at the Fredonian outbreak in 1826. Though Santa Anna and Bustamente were in the death struggle for the mastery of Mexico, both parties and all factions took a moment's armistice at the receipt of the ill news of the uprising in Texas. Teran had remained true to Bustamente and commanded his forces in the Eastern Division. Santa Anna sent Montezuma to assume command in that Division, and a battle between him and Teran, fought in 1823, gave Montezuma the advantage. Teran saw the sure success of Santa Anna, and ill news was coming to him from Texas, all his worst fears now came upon him, and this talented and valiant man fell on his sword at Perdillo, in June, 1832. Montezuma assumed charge of affairs in the Eastern Division, in the name of Santa Anna, and since this Division included Texas, he gave anxious heed to the wild rumors of rebellion which came thick and fast from Texas, in the midsummer of that year.

Like all the other Mexican leaders, he assumed that the long looked for rebellion had come to pass in Texas, and he saw behind it the wicked schemes of the United States of the North. A temporary truce was arranged between the warring factions in Mexico, who were so strenuously striving for each other's utter extermination, while Montezuma organized and dispatched a strong detachment to quell the rebellion in Texas.

Colonel Jose Antonio Mexia left Tampico in July with a squadron of six ships and four hundred men and with plenary powers to restore order and Mexican sovereignty in Texas. As he came past Matamoros, he stopped to confer with his arch enemy, Colonel Manzamores, who still held that small corner of the earth for Bustamente, and that worthy bade Mexia God-speed in his crusade against the common enemy.

During these troubled days, Stephen F. Austin was down at Saltillo, in Coahuila, where he was attending a session of the Legislature, of which he was a member from Texas. Poor Austin was not in sympathy with many of the hot-headed leaders in Texas, who were bent on war and separation from Mexico. He had been absent from home some weeks and had not followed the trend of events. He was picked up at Matamoros by Mexia's fleet and came on with them to the mouth of the Brazos, which they reached on July 20th, a few weeks after the battle of Velasco. This afforded Austin a splendid opportunity to impress upon Mexia his fidelity to Mexico, and as was ever the case where the Mexican leaders viewed Texas through an acquaintance with Austin, the impression of Texas and the Texans was decidedly improved.

The approach of Mexia's fleet, supposed to bring with it the ire of Mexico, seemed to forebode dark days for the colonists, and indeed there was much apprehension throughout the country during these summer days of 1832.

Colonel John Austin, Admiral William J. Russell, William H. Wharton, and others who were awaiting the coming of Mexia's fleet, artfully met the situation by hastening to meet and receive the Colonel as an accredited envoy of Santa Anna, for whom they proclaimed in loud terms. In order to duly impress Mexia with their sincerity, they organized a mass meeting at Brazoria and with much ceremony read in a loud tone of voice the "blessed Turtle Bayou Resolutions."

Stephen Austin and Colonel Mexia were everywhere received with transports of great joy and were wined and dined up and down the Brazos. A banquet of great dimensions was held at the plantation home of William H. Wharton, at Eagle Island, just below Brazoria, where there was rhetoric, both in Spanish and English, and music, and many good things to drink. Under these felicitous environments, they gave cheers for Santa Anna and the constitution of 1824, of which he was heralded as the champion and preserver. Of course they did not know that in trading Bustamente for Santa Anna, they had swapped the devil for the witch, or possibly I should say the witch for the devil, but at any rate this turn of affairs gave the colonists a respite of three or four years, during which many things happened to improve their situation and opportunities for successful resistance.

Colonel Mexia visited San Felipe and Nacogdoches and other points in Texas and finding everywhere prepared evidences of loyalty and devotion to Mexico and to the constitution of 1824, and especially to Santa Anna, he went home happy. One cannot but wonder what would have been the result had this good natured, hard drinking Mexican Colonel been a man of Teran's ability and foresight, but "God moves in a mysterious way, His wonders to perform."

Though Colonel Mexia was in those days a champion of Santa Anna, things changed about in later years, and in 1839 he lead an expedition outfitted largely at New Orleans against Santa Anna, who was again in power.

At the battle of Heajete, near Pueblo, he was defeated and captured, and Santa Anna sentenced him to be shot in half an hour. "He is very kind," said General Mexia, "had I taken him I would have shot him in five minutes."

THE REVOLUTION

Antonio Lopez de Santa Anna

It is Eighteen Hundred and Thirty-Two. The scenes are now set for the great drama of the Revolution. It has been ten years since Austin and his little company of first colonists camped on New Year's Creek and since William Morton burned away the cane brake and planted the first corn crop on the banks of the Brazos across from where Richmond now stands. Yet these ten years have seen wondrous changes. In 1832 there were 30,000 people in Texas, settled all the way from the Sabine to the Guadalupe, all for independence from Mexico, and many of them intemperate and outspoken in their plans and purposes. They had a contempt for the prudence and patience of Austin and were open in their criticism of him.

As we are about to study this very important quadrennial, 1832 to 1836, it is interesting to sketch an outline of some of the remarkable characters who played upon this stage. Biography must ever be one of the most important forms of literature and history, for what is more interesting to men than the romantic relation of the deeds of other men of action who have been upon this mortal stage before we came to play our petty parts?

Of the many names we encounter in the drama of the Revolution none is heard more often than that of Antonio Lopez de Santa Anna, who was born in Jalapa, Mexico, in 1795, and who died in the City of Mexico in his eighty-second year, in 1876. Few men have had a more interesting and varied career. He entered the Spanish army at fifteen, and fought against the patriot cause until he saw the finish of Spanish sovereignty in 1821, when he, like Iturbide, turned patriot. He supported Iturbide at first, but as soon as that person came into power Santa Anna began to plot against him, for plotting was ever his chief enterprise. As early as December, 1822, he openly revolted and led the revolution which overthrew the empire and sent Iturbide into exile. At the close of Victoria's term (he being the first constitutional president), Santa Anna led a second revolution against the seating of Gomez Pedraza, who had been declared elected by Congress to succeed Victoria, and this revolution resulted in having Pedraza driven out. Santa Anna played a leading part in placing the patriot Guerrera in power instead of Pedraza. This was in 1828.

The following year the Spanish government made a last feeble attempt to reconquer Mexico, and landed a force at Vera Cruz. Santa Anna led an army against the Spaniards and defeated them, earning for himself the plaudits of his country. It was currently rumored that he had in fact assembled this force to overthrow Guerrera, whom he had only a few months before placed in the presidency; but the Spanish invasion gave him a timely pretense to turn his revolutionary designs into patriotic purposes. After his military success against the Spaniards he retired to his estate at Jalapa, but renewed or continued his intrigues against Guerrera. But Bustamente beat him to the next revolution and made himself president in 1829. Naturally, and very promptly, Santa Anna now turned his attention and his designs to Bustamente, for he was perfectly impartial in his plotting and consistently contrived against all persons in power.

In January, 1832, he declared openly against the government of Bustamente and led the revolution which culminated in this year, the effects of which were felt throughout Texas. After his defeat of Bustamente in December, 1832, he had himself elected president along with Gomez Farias, vice-president. Instead of going to the capital and assuming the duties of the Chief Magistracy, this strange, intriguing person invested Gomez Farias, the vice-president, with supreme power and again retired to his estates in Jalapa to plot against his own administration. His love of duplicity and intrigue were so great that he relished such a role more than the realization of supreme power. Then, too, he had in his campaign against Bustamente posed as champion of constitutional government and had allowed his name to be linked with a desire to restore the constitution of 1824.

This he had no notion of doing, and he did not dare unmask at once after his elevation. Between 1832 and 1834, while he was president in retirement, he actively engaged in several campaigns against spasmodic insurrections here and there, always keeping the control of such military organization as the country possessed. In 1834 he would resume the presidency, but though he were the lawful president and had the right to leave his estate and come into the city and become president, yet force of habit was so strong with him that he preferred to do so through the medium of a revolution.

So he led an insurrection against his vice-president, Gomez Farias, and took active charge of the government. During the two years he had been president in retirement, he had allowed all the odium of misgovernment to accumulate against Farias. In January, 1835, he had himself declared president by the Mexican Congress, but almost immediately retired to his Jalapa plantation and arranged for General Barragan to act as provisional president. He probably hoped that it would be necessary to hatch a plot and start a revolution to put Barragan out. From his estate in Jalapa he continued to arrange a plan by which he would at the right time become absolute ruler of Mexico, and gradually, but thoroughly, he had all forms of constitutional government abolished, dismantled the state governments to the extent that the governors were to be appointed by, and dependent upon, him, and scrapped the constitution.

Some of the state governments resisted the open attempt at subversion and stood out against him. Coahuila was one of the last to fall. All hope that he would protect the constitution of 1824 was now gone, the mask was off;

and in 1835 Texans knew that the hour had struck. This was the man whom they hailed as their deliverer in 1832, and whom they faced and fought as a tyrant in 1836.

It would be interesting indeed to follow the forty years of his career after the Texas Campaign but this is the history of Mexico for four decades.

Whatever else may be said of him we must concede that he was a most remarkable man.

THE FIRST TEXAS CONVENTION OF OCTOBER, 1832

We come now to the interesting epoch when the people of Texas first began to assemble in convention and to discuss the common weal. The mass meeting and convention, as these institutions had developed in the States, had become a powerful medium of free speech. Such institutions were unknown among the Latin people. In Mexico and the other Spanish-American countries, a mass meeting where men assemble and discuss principles without coming to blows, was unknown and impossible. In August, 1832, Horatio Chrisman, first alcalde of San Felipe, joined John Austin, the second alcalde, in a call for a general convention of all the colonies of Texas. The call indicated that it was to discuss the misrepresentations that had been circulated concerning the purposes of Texas in driving out the garrisons in 1832. The people wanted to go on record against the rumor that Texas sought independence and to give some public declaration of fealty to Mexico. It was also stated in the call there was to be a discussion of Indian affairs. Fifty-six delegates from sixteen districts assembled at San Felipe, on the Brazos, Bexar alone being unrepresented.

The Mexican population of San Antonio could not be induced to join in such enterprise. Austin and William H. Wharton were nominated to preside over the convention and Austin was chosen president. The delegates came all the way from the Sabine to Bastrop. When the convention assembled it was discovered that there was a well divided and well-balanced division of sentiment, there being a radical party that secretly favored independence though they openly avowed the contrary, and a very conservative party that did not favor separation from Mexico. Austin was in all respects the soul and leader of the conservatives. The Whartons were the representatives and leaders of the more radical element.

The first topic which came up for discussion was the decree of 1830, which prevented the further settlement of Americans in Texas. This had been the severest trial to the colonists of all of the Mexican decrees. Though it had been generally disregarded and people from the States came freely during the period from 1830 to 1832, yet the fact that they were denied the privilege of coming and acquiring a status of citizenship was a matter of grave concern to the colonists. A committee of five was appointed to prepare a memorial to the Mexican Republic praying for a repeal of the exclusion law and to set forth the trials and dangers encountered in efforts to colonize the country, and to emphasize the respect and attachment that the people bore for the constitution and laws of the Republic.

William H. Wharton was made chairman of this committee and wrote its report. An executive committee was appointed to draft a petition for the reduction of the duties on necessities. Another committee composed of Luke Leassier, William McFarland, William Menefee, Samuel Bruff and Thomas Hastings was appointed to prepare a petition to the state government for a donation of land to Texas for the creation of a school fund for the maintenance of primary schools. This is probably the first legislation, if it may be so called, bearing upon the topic of public schools, that was ever formulated in Texas. But it must be remembered that this is the first public representative assemblage that was ever held in Texas. The question uppermost in the minds of those who sat in this convention was that of separate statehood for Texas. It was discussed informally, and there was an effort made to keep it from being brought before the convention because there were those who foresaw that a move in this direction would mean trouble. On the third day, however, it was presented and debated with much interest. A vote of 36 to 12 was registered in favor of appointing a committee of two from each municipality to report the expediency of petitioning for a state government. A memorial requesting a separate state government was prepared, and William H. Wharton was chosen messenger to present it, and it was suggested that Juan Raphael Monchola, of Goliad, accompany him. It was never, however, formally presented, and the question came up again in 1833, and again in 1834, when Austin went to Mexico to present such memorial and was imprisoned for treason for having done so.

After a six-day session the convention adjourned. Before doing so, however, it appointed a standing central committee in San Felipe which was to be subordinate to the local committees in the districts represented in the convention. F. W. Johnson, whose name is indeed conspicuous during the revolutionary period, was made chairman of this central committee with authority to call another convention, if necessary. The memorial requesting separate statehood was couched in the most respectful and genteel terms; its language was selected and guarded. Yet strange it may seem, not only the Mexican authorities but the Mexican citizens of Texas looked upon this simple, respectful petition as a declaration of war and as treason of the first order. The political chief at San Antonio, Don Jose de la Garza, wrote the governor of Coahuila referring to it as a wide-spreading insurrection, and suggested, "that a true Mexican could but bitterly deplore his misfortune and feel sore at the foreign hand that had come boldly to rob him of his rights, employing physical force when even rational arguments from such a source ought hardly be tolerated." No clearer glimpse of the Mexican mind can be shown than these chance expressions found in Garza's letter. A Mexican could not understand how it were possible that there would be such a thing as a lawful loyal assemblage to voice public sentiment. Such a thing seemed as paradoxical to him as a lawful riot or a peaceful fight. To him all such meetings were per se treasonable and revolutionary.

The central committee provided by this convention was the first state governmental machinery devised in Texas. Through it another convention was called the following year.

THE CONVENTION OF 1833

The news of the San Felipe Convention of 1832 produced as great a commotion in Mexican political circles as the Fredonian Rebellion had done six years before. All official Mexico regarded it as seditious and treasonable that the colonists should assemble in a public place and state their grievances. The patriotic utterances found in the journal of the convention seemed to have been accepted as a challenge to Mexican sovereignty. When the matter was called to the attention of Santa Anna, who was at the moment in supreme authority in Mexico, he wrote: "I am satisfied that the foreigners who have intruded themselves into the province of Texas have a strong tendency to declare themselves independent of the republic, and their remonstrances and complaints are but disguised to that end." He suggested that General Filisola be sent into Texas with a sufficient force "to secure the integrity of our territory."

The Minister of State wrote the political chief at San Antonio: "Your Lordship will make use of all means in your power to cause these Texans to understand that such excesses among them as have recently come to light must inevitably bring ruin upon them." In the meanwhile the colonists were utterly oblivious to the storm that the San Felipe Convention of 1832 had produced in far away

Mexico, called and planned the second convention of all Texas, which assembled at San Felipe on the Brazos in 1833. The central committee which had been constituted by the convention the year before, issued the call in January. This second convention was in many respects a repetition of the first.

About the same number of delegates attended. Austin and Wharton were again candidates for the presidency or chairmanship of the convention, and this time Wharton was chosen, showing a tendency towards a more radical course. Sam Houston appeared in this convention as a delegate from San Augustine, and this was his first appearance and participation in public affairs in Texas. The convention the year before had approached the question of separate statehood delicately and declared for it, and pointed out provisions of the constitution of Coahuila and Texas which had been adopted in 1827, which justified the setting up of a separate state government in Texas. These provisions declared that as soon as Texas should be in a condition to form a state it should make a declaration to that effect to Congress for further action. The Convention of 1832 and the one of 1833 seemed, therefore, to have been following this constitutional provision, and neither did more than to make a declaration in favor of separate statehood.

The Convention of 1833 went so far as to propose a constitution for the new state. Stephen F. Austin and James B. Miller, of Gonzales, and Don Erasmo Seguin, the same urbane gentlemen who had been sent twelve years before to welcome Austin to Texas, were appointed messengers to bear this petition to Mexico. Austin alone went on this perilous mission, leaving Texas early in May, 1833. His good faith and the good faith of his people seemed sufficient to guarantee the integrity of his enterprise. The people of Texas did not know the effect that these conventions had upon the Mexican mind, else this journey never would have been undertaken.

The most interesting thing which this convention did was to form a proposed constitution for the proposed state.

The document is yet in existence and is the first of our many constitutions. It contains a clause declaring that no bank shall be established in Texas for 99 years. It is said that Dr. Archer proposed a plan for creation of a state bank, and that Sam Houston led the opposition to it. This was but a reflex of the fight that had been raging in the States, and that yet raged on during the Jackson administration over the Bank of the United States.

We all know that Jackson's fight on the bank was the result of one of his petty prejudices and not from any principle. But it became a conviction with him, one of his very articles of faith, and he kept on with the fight until he destroyed the bank and the credit of the country, and brought on our first real financial panic. Houston was in all things a devotee and follower of General Jackson, and on his first opportunity in Texas he began a Jackson fight on the phantom bank which was proposed for incorporation in the proposed constitution. His arguments against the bank prevailed, and it was outlawed for 99 years. As long as Houston dominated in Texas affairs, there was no banking system, nor were there any banks in Texas until long after it became a state in the American union.

Austin's Second Journey to Mexico, in May 1833

Eleven years had elapsed since Austin, a youth only twenty-eight years old, had made his first visit to Mexico and had gotten a confirmation of his father's colonial grant. He had spent these years between in unremitting toil and had seen his colonial enterprise prosper and flourish. It was against his judgment that he undertook the mission thrust upon him by the Convention of 1833, but he knew that no one else in Texas could do so with any assurance of success. At Matamoros he had an interview with General Filisola and was reassured by that gentleman, who advised Austin that he was about to re-establish military garrisons in Texas to enforce the revenue laws. After this conference, Austin wrote back to Brazoria: "I have pledged my honor that Filisola would have the full support of Texas in sustaining the law, and I have full confidence that the people will not forget my pledge." This letter was written just before he took passage for Vera Cruz and he assures his people of his faith in the Mexican government. He reached the City of Mexico in June, 1833, in the midst of a terrible epidemic of cholera.

After a long time he was able to present the memorial of the San Felipe Convention of 1833 to the Mexican Congress, then in session, and he labored through the whole summer in an effort to get some recognition of the plans for separate statehood. He did succeed in getting a revocation of the Decree of 1830 forbidding further emigration from the States, and when we understand the circumstances it is marvelous that he accomplished this much. He continued his labors until December of 1833, and was now convinced that Santa Anna was at heart a despot and that Congress would deny to Texas a separate statehood. He had not received the warm hand of cordial treatment that he had been accorded in Mexican official circles on his former visit to the city. He found a general distrust against the Texans, and especially the people and the government of the United States. He then suspected and we now know, that this was in part brought about by the conduct of the American Minister to Mexico.

The Adams administration had sent Joel Poinsette of South Carolina as Minister to Mexico, and had caused him to labor unceasingly for the purchase of Texas. Although his plan of procedure was not always commendable, yet there was nothing particularly vicious or unseemly about it. But with the incoming of the Jackson administration and the spoils system of public office which General Jackson introduced, some strange personalities got into power, not only in Washington but everywhere that political intrigue could succeed in naming an office-seeker to place. One Anthony Butler had been made representative to Mexico, and a student of Mexican and American history, after the lapse of nearly a hundred years, is brought to blush at the infamy of this individual. He intrigued against every government that prevailed in Mexico during his stay there.

He intrigued against Texas and the Texans, and he helped circulate false rumors about Austin, and probably contributed largely to the failure of Austin's mission, and to his subsequent imprisonment. Shortly before leaving the City of Mexico for his return home, Austin addressed a letter to the ayuntamiento at San Antonio urging the people of that jurisdiction to join the other districts of Texas in requesting separate statehood. He, no doubt, felt that if the Mexican population of San Antonio would join the other colonies in such a request that it would have weight; and he also felt some chagrin that the San Antonio people withheld their influence in this matter. This letter contained an expression that was a little injudicious. He wrote: "All the municipalities of Texas should come without delay to an understanding and arrange a local government for Texas as a state of the Mexican Federation. Things should be prepared with harmony, thus being ready for the time when the Congress will refuse approval." He left the City of Mexico December 10th. This letter which he had dispatched to San Antonio in October was promptly returned to the City of Mexico, and as soon as its contents were made known to the government officials there, orders were issued for Austin's arrest, and he was overtaken at Saltillo and apprehended and carried back to the City of Mexico and incarcerated in a dungeon which had been left over from the Spanish Inquisition.

AUSTIN IN PRISON

Austin has left among his papers a diary beginning with the day he left the City of Mexico, on December 10th, and covering a large part of the time that he was in prison. He probably wrote his diary during the latter part of his imprisonment, when he was allowed some liberty and subjected to less scrutiny. The first pages indicate that they may have been written upon the dates they bear, as they give no intimation of his impending arrest. He left the City of Mexico traveling in a coach with several well known gentlemen. The party was in constant apprehension of brigands and went well armed. On December 16th they reached Quaretero, where thirty years later Maximilian met his fate. He spent the day there and visited the churches and other places of interest. That he had no forewarning of the danger that awaited him seems obvious from the following taken from his diary covering his stay in Quaretero:

16th December.

We remain in Quaretero; visited convents. There are many and very large. One has a large fountain constructed by a marquis who has perpetuated his fame and piety by a statue of himself of his own size which stands in the center of the fountain on the base of stone. There are extensive baths convenient to this fountain constructed by this same marquis. One wonders how much sweat and tears from the Indian slaves it cost which the marquis employed in the construction of this fountain and baths, but he received absolution from the monks and went to heaven. In the orchard there are many pretty cypress trees. I collected seeds from them to carry to Texas. They showed me some of these trees planted by the hands of Rev. Father Morfit, who had been a monk in this convent and was at one time a missionary at Nacogdoches, in Texas. This monk is very famous, for he has been a second Moses. At Nacogdoches all the springs went dry and he went out with images of the saints and necessary apparatus to perform miracles. He struck a blow with a rod of iron on a rock which stands on the bank of Lanana Creek in Nacogdoches and immediately a stream of water gushed out sufficient to supply the inhabitants with water to drink. This miracle was canonized in Rome and a print of engraving of the Father was made. This same padre, when he left Nacogdoches for Bexar, lost a baggage mule which a tiger killed, and in the morning as soon as the padre knew it he made the tiger come and kneel at his feet and then he was harnessed and loaded with the baggage of the dead mule, which he carried to Bexar, and then having received a pardon for having killed the mule was sent back to the desert. All this is true because several old women told it to me in Nacogdoches and in Bexar and we ought never to suppose that Rome would order an engraving to be made of the miracle of the water only to deceive credulous people.

The journal continues with this same delightful narrative until his arrival at Saltillo on February 3rd, when it contains the simple memorandum;

On the third day I was arrested by General Lemus by orders from the Secretary of War, dated in Mexico, December 21st.

Daily entries covered the return to the City of Mexico.

February 13th: In Mexico, where I was put in the Inquisition, shut up in the dark dungeon I am not allowed communication with anyone.

February 14th: Heard cannon fire during the day in memory of Guerrera, who was shot on this day, 1831.

The entry of February 20th is interesting and has since caused much comment:

> Is it or not the interest of Texas to separate herself even if she were at liberty to do so? No, certainly not. Is it or not the interest of the United States of the North to acquire Texas? It is not, because she would extend her territory too much. And what is worse? She would annex a large district which would have no interest in common with the rest of the republic. All the rivers of Texas take their rise in Texas at a little distance from each other and do not enter the territories of the north so as to form bonds of union as does the River Mississippi in Louisiana and other States adjacent. There is no market in the north for the produce of Texas, and there is in Mexico. Texas is more distant to the seat of Washington than from the City of Mexico. As regards the trade with Europe, the Mexican flag is equal to that of the north. What then is the true interest of Texas? It is to have local Government, to cement and strengthen its union with Mexico instead of weakening or breaking it. What Texas wants is an organization of a local government, and it is of little consequence whether it be a part of Coahuila or a separate State or Territory, provided the organization he a suitable one.

Whether Austin expressed his real sentiments or whether he was writing this for the eye of his inquisitors has been a matter of much speculation, but I am inclined to believe that he meant what he wrote, for I do not think that he was capable of duplicity even though he were in the dungeon of the Inquisition facing trial for treason.

> February 26th. What a horrible punishment is solitary confinement, shut up in a dungeon with scarcely light enough to distinguish anything! If I were a criminal it would be another thing, but I am not one.

I have been ensnared and precipitated, but my intentions were pure and correct.

February 23rd: Philanthropy is but another name of trouble. I have labored with pure intentions to benefit others, and especially to advance and improve my adopted country. What have I gained? Enemies, persecution, imprisonment, accused of ingratitude to Mexico, which is one of the most unjust accusations which can be brought against me.

There are many things in this interesting diary which every Texan should read. Broken in health from the arduous labors of the last decade, and now confined in this dark, solitary dungeon, poor Austin indeed had a right to feel that his philanthropy was the cause of all his troubles.

EIGHTEEN HUNDRED THIRTY-FOUR

There was no convention or general assembly in Texas this year. Austin's imprisonment had cast a gloom over the colonies. There had been high hopes that when he reached Mexico bearing the worthy memorials of the San Felipe Convention of 1833, that the difficulties of Texas would find solution.

To all thoughtful men his incarceration was the last challenge, but both popular expression and open action were arrested for fear that any action or outburst in Texas would cost Austin his life. In the meantime every semblance of state government in Texas and Coahuila was going to pieces. There was a civil war raging in Coahuila between two factions, one declaring that Saltillo was the capital of the state and the other holding forth at Monclova.

Oliver Jones was the delegate from Texas to the state congress or legislature, and in September he wrote from Monclova that the state government was gone and that anarchy prevailed. Though Texas had no state government, yet the people of the colonies were industrious and orderly and the local ayuntemientos in the different districts furnished a substantial local government for the time being. The year before the state had been divided into the departments of Brazos and Nacogdoches, and Henry Smith of Brazoria had been named political chief of the Department of Brazos, he being the first American honored with such an appointment. His elevation placed him in leadership during the absence of Austin. Upon the receipt of Jones' letter, Smith issued a long address, the gist of which was, that since there was no state government in Coahuila, and since Texas must have a government, therefore it should take the initiative and organize one. He suggested another convention. Henry Smith was indeed a worthy patriot. The year following he was chosen Provisional Governor of Texas, and the portrait of the old frontiersman hangs in our state capitol today as the first of the American governors of Texas. But as a political leader in troublesome times, he was a sad failure.

The people of Bexar had never cooperated with the other colonies in any movement looking to the common good, but there were some splendid men among the Mexican citizens there. Seguin wrote Smith this year suggesting a convention at Bexar. Since this was the first time that any offer of cooperation had been made from that source, the invitation was seized upon, and there was for a time considerable hope that a convention could be held at San Antonio which could probably find avenues of access to Mexican political life not open from San Felipe. The people of San Antonio, however, did not act upon the suggestion and nothing definite came of it.

In the meanwhile Juan Nepomuceno Almonte, a brilliant Mexican officer and leader, well known in that day and generation, visited the colonies as the representative of Santa Anna and assured the people of the benevolence of this great republican chieftain. Almonte came again to Texas in 1836 and was in the battle of San Jacinto. A Mexican subaltern who afterwards wrote an account of the battle, says that when he reached a bayou where the fleeing Mexican soldiers were struggling to get across, that he saw Almonte plunge into the water and swim across holding his sword in his hand above the water as though to keep it dry. A few days following the battle, a Texas lad picked up a sword on the bank of the bayou and in years later a son of this boy, then a very old man, gave me the sword, and I have it. It may be Almonte's sword, but it may not.

At the time of his first visit to Texas in 1834, he was only thirty years old, and was a man of splendid appearance and address, was just entering upon a long, stormy career in Mexican political life. Almonte was the natural son of the Mexican patriot priest Morelos, who started a revolution for independence against Spain in 1811. On one occasion when there was grave doubt as to the fidelity of his followers, Morelos appeared before a mass meeting or mob and tried to make an address. As soon as he came and looked into the faces of those around him, he saw his doom. Standing at a distance in the audience he saw the eager face of his son, for whom he had a deep affection. Pointing to the youth he exclaimed shrilly, "Almonte, Almonte" (to the mountain; to the mountain). He was warning the lad to flee for his life, and the boy made his escape. And when this genial gentleman came to a man's estate he carried with him the name Almonte with which he was thus tragically christened.

When Waddy Thompson was American minister to Mexico in the forties, he became a close friend of Almonte, and often visited in his home, where he saw the portrait of Morelos, represented in the uniform of a Mexican general, but with the priest's mitre on his head. Almonte was active in Mexican political affairs for thirty years and went down with the ill-fated empire in the late sixties. While he was in Texas in 1834, Austin was in prison in

Mexico, and he promised his assistance for his liberation upon his return, and it is said he made his promise good.

On October 5, 1834, Santa Anna called a council to discuss the state of affairs in Texas. Among those present were Lorenza de Zavala, then high in Mexican official circles and about to be sent as minister to France, and they brought Austin out of prison to sit in this council. Santa Anna, with his usual urbanity, treated Austin with great consideration, and Texas' affairs were discussed with considerable freedom. It was, however, decided that Texas should remain attached to Coahuila, and Austin was sent back to prison. It was also decided at this conference to send a garrison of four thousand troops to Texas to keep away the Indians. The end of this year found Texas without a government and Austin yet in prison.

THE LAND SCANDALS OF 1835

The year 1835 was an unhappy and turbulent one in Texas. Austin was still in prison. By midsummer all semblance of Mexican authority had disappeared from the colonies. The state government down in Coahuila had been torn into rival factions openly at war with each other, and this furnished some pretext for Santa Anna's intervention. Before the state legislature was entirely suppressed, it loaned itself to a series of land acts which were the legislative scandal of those days, and which have come down to us with a forbidding odor even after nearly one hundred years.

We find in these "land grabbing" enterprises the names of some of our most sterling patriots. It is a story as old as Egypt, for:

> *Who can doubt the secret hid*
> *Under Cheops pyramid,*
> *Is that the contractor did*
> *Cheops out of several million?"*

Land speculation was rife in those days and the millions of acres of open domain which lay unclaimed was a temptation which would have mislead any generation of our ancestors and which might even tempt us today. But it must be remembered that the acquisition of real estate has ever been one of the strong characteristics of our tribe. There is a story of how two itinerant Saxon Chiefs came to North England centuries ago and bought an ox-hide of earth, and how they cut the oxhide in strips and in the rainy season stretched it around what is now a large part of an English shire.

Well, the oxhide trick was worked overtime down at Monclova in 1834 and 1835.

In the colonization law of 1825, there was a provision which was construed to give the state government authority to sell land to Mexicans upon such terms as it might see fit, as much as eleven leagues of land in a single grant. *Eleven leagues of land*—how that term sounds to us who have seen a city lot sell for five hundred dollars a front foot, or a single oil acre for tens of thousands. *Eleven leagues of land*; this is nearly fifty thousand English acres. Enterprising Mexicans were not long in learning of this privilege, and soon after its passage, one Juan Antonio Padilla procured the first grant, which was located in 1828. There were numerous grants which sold for as low as $100.00 per league. In 1830, the patriot James Bowie, who is said to have been the inventor and a skillful operator of the knife which bears his name, journeyed down to Saltillo and induced various Mexicans residing there to apply for eleven league grants, and when they had been made Bowie purchased the certificates and they were trafficked about and locations were made under them. These transactions much disturbed many of the colonies, for the locations under these large grants bearing Mexican names often conflicted with the little land holdings of a stockman farmer who only had a petty league and labor.

They threatened to hinder Ben Milam's Red River Colony in a serious way, and he undertook a trip to Mexico in 1834 to protest against them; and was returning from that long perilous journey in '35 when he joined the patriot army on its way to Bexar. In the troubled days of 1834 and '5, when the state government of Coahuila was in confusion, there were a series of these acts which reflect no credit upon the times.

In 1834, an act was passed designed to grant a bounty to soldiers who would enlist for service against the Indians, and under this act Samuel M. Williams, Robert Peeples and F. W. Johnson obtained a grant for one hundred leagues. The last legislature which met in '35 was unusually active in this regard. An act was passed on March 14th, which gave the governor authority in the "present emergency" to dispose of lands about as he saw fit, and under it, certificates for about 400 leagues were issued.

S. M. Williams and John Durst got one hundred and twenty-four of these certificates which they resold. The last of these land statutes were passed in April, 1835, just before Cos' army reached Monclova on its march north for Texas via Coahuila. It was known that the army was approaching with authority to suppress the legislature, and in its dying hours on April 7th, it passed a final enactment which gave the governor yet more authority to sell land.

Doctor James Grant, who perished in the Revolution only a few months later, came away with certificates for 100 leagues which he sold and after his death his estate listed unlocated and unsold certificates for 300 leagues. As Cos' army approached there was a wild exodus of legislators and land speculators.

Governor Viesca decided to cast his lot with the Texans and left for the Rio Grande along with a company of Texans who rode out of Monclova just before the Mexican army rode in.

These land transactions were seized upon by Santa Anna as a cause for his attitude towards the state government of Coahuila and the Texans. It was declaimed that a corrupt Mexican legislature connived with a worse coterie of Texans in schemes to exploit the public domain, and that severe military measures were necessary to prevent these wholesale frauds. Hence these land speculations are often given as one of the causes of the Revolution, though in fact we know they were an incident rather than a cause. But nowhere were they more severely condemned than in Texas. Almost every public gathering during 1834 and '35 denounced them in terrible terms. The provisional government organized at San Felipe in the autumn of 1835, closed the land office until affairs should become more settled. The congress of the Republic in 1840 conducted a thorough investigation of these so-called land frauds, and a vast amount of information was gathered and much of it written in the legislative journals.

But for the most part those whose names were connected with these ventures, earned absolution in the Revolution.

Bowie fell at the Alamo, Grant at Refugio; Frank Johnson was in the siege of Bexar. They were not bad men merely because they coveted land in large quantities.

Their bones are dust,
Their good swords rust,
Their souls are with the saints,
We trust.

GONZALES

After reducing the state government in Coahuila General Cos came on to Bexar with a considerable army, where he stationed himself among fairly congenial Mexican population. Through the military authorities there, an order was issued for the arrest of some of the more outspoken men in the colonies for seditious utterances. R. M. Williamson (Three-legged Willie), had made a very patriotic 4th of July address which was considered treasonable. Colonel Travis had lead a small force which had forcibly expelled the Mexican garrison at Anahuac in July. Lorenza De Zavala had fled from Mexico and taken up his residence on Buffalo Bayou below Harrisburg. These men and others were to be arrested and sent to Mexico for trial. Some letters which were sent from Cos to Colonel Ugartechea told of active plans to punish the colonies, and all was at white heat as the early autumn approached. A general consultation was called to meet at San Felipe in October. The militia was being organized everywhere, and no man now doubted that war to the death was inevitable. Amid these stirring scenes so full of apprehensions when the convention was about to assemble and men were everywhere leaving their homes for military service, a tremendous comet suddenly appeared and filled the evening skies with a weird, sinister light.

In the lonely plantation homes where the husband and father was away in the gathering army this strange astral wanderer left a feeling of terror and awe which was daily augmented by the wildest rumors of Mexican invasion and Indian uprisings.

The storm broke down at Gonzales in October, when Colonel Ugartechea, the same who was driven out of Velasco in 1832, came with a small detachment of men to take away a cannon which the government had furnished the settlement some years before for defense against the Indians. Anticipating this attempt several hundred Tex-

ans had hurriedly gathered, and the first skirmish, sometimes called our Lexington, resulted in the very hurried
return of the Mexicans to Bexar without the cannon.

There were stirring scenes on the Guadalupe in these
October days. Colonel John H. Moore with a company of
men from La Grange was among the first to arrive. Fannin was there with the Brazoria guards. R. M. Coleman
was there with men from Bastrop. A small detachment
from the Colorado under Thomas Alley were the first to
come. Austin, who had been released from prison a few
months before, had landed at the mouth of the Brazos in
September, and had ridden by San Felipe, thence on to
Gonzales, where he arrived on October 10th.

The two Whartons, Wm. J. Russell and Wm. H. Jack
came across from Brazoria. Years later Russell told of an
interesting incident he witnessed between Austin and
Wm. H. Wharton. They had been estranged and for some
years were not on speaking terms. Wharton had been a
bitter critic of Austin and had attacked his pacific policies
in public print.

When Russell and Wharton reached the log house in
Gonzales where they were to spend the night, they were
told that Colonel Austin had preceded them a few hours
and was in the next room. Russell, with Wharton's permission, went in to speak with Austin and offer reconcil-
iation.

He says that when he entered the room Austin was lying on a blanket utterly exhausted from a long day's ride
in the rain, that his thin, pale face showed ghastly in the
faint light of a candle by which he was writing.

The buoyant boy who fourteen years before had ridden
to Bexar to begin his colonial enterprise was at forty-one
a broken, dying man. When Russell addressed him he
was glad to forget all differences and in almost sepulchral
voice bemoaned the plight of "poor Texas."

The next day they chose him commander-in-chief of the
"Federal Army." When he was returning to Texas from

his first visit to Mexico in 1823, the military commandant at Monterey had commissioned him a Lieutenant Colonel so that during the colonial days he had been Colonel Austin. He was now General Austin, with an army of 600 men, and the first order he issued on the day of his election was to cross the Guadalupe and on to Bexar.

The most interesting picture of these Gonzales days that has come to us is found in the delightful narrative of Noah Smithwick, a young man who was one of these volunteers, and marched with them to San Antonio. Sixty years later the old man dictated his recollections to his daughter, who wrote in pleasing style, and they have given the most interesting sketch of that period which has come down to us.

The remainder of this article is literally quoted from Smithwick's recollections:

> Colonel Milam joined us at Gonzales. He had recently escaped a Mexican prison and his wardrobe was much depleted. He was more than six feet and his pantaloons and sleeves were far too short for his stature. Buckskin breeches were the nearest approach to uniform, and they were of every variety and complexion—some too short, others too long. Here a broad brimmed sombrero overshadowed a military cap and a tall bee gum would ride along with a coonskin cap with tail hanging down behind as all well regulated tails should do. Here a big American horse loomed above a Spanish pony or a skittish mustang pranced along with a methodical mule. Here a bulky roll of quilts jostled a bundle of blankets or more apt a buffalo robe, or a gaudy counterpane woven by tender hands with no shadow of presentiment that it should be a winding sheet.

> In lieu of canteens each soldier carried a Spanish gourd. So with the old cannon flag flying and the artillery (the one cannon) mounted on a wooden wheeled wagon driven by teams of oxen, we filed out

of Gonzales and took up our march on to San Antonio. At the Cibola Creek, Sam Houston came up with us. It was my first sight of him. I have a vivid picture of him now as he rode into our camp alone mounted on a small yellow Spanish stallion, his feet almost touching the ground. He almost immediately returned to San Felipe to attend the convention.

And now we must leave the buckskin army on its way to Bexar and foregather with those who sat in the consultation.

THE CONSULTATION

In the midsummer of 1835, the local Committee of Safety at San Felipe had proposed that each jurisdiction throughout Texas send one member to San Felipe, and that these members compose a temporary committee of safety pending the general convention which was to assemble in the autumn. This suggestion was acted upon, and R. R. Royal of Matagorda was chosen to preside over this council. It acted as a kind of clearinghouse for revolutionary activities and was the nearest approach to a governmental body which prevailed in the interim.

When the consultation met and was organized, the General Council, as the central committee was called, wound up its affairs and made a final report to the convention, which assumed governmental functions.

It met on October 15th, but was adjourned from day to day to November 1st, awaiting the arrival of the delegations. R. R. Royal called the convention to order, and on motion of Sam Houston, of Nacogdoches, Dr. Branch T. Archer was chosen to preside.

It fell his lot to make what we now call the keynote speech, which he did without unnecessary rhetoric. His address is copied in the journal of the consultation, and one reading it now after the lapse of years is impressed with its calm dignity. He recommended,

(a) A declaration of causes.
(b) The organization of a provisional government.
(c) A military organization.
(d) A conciliatory arrangement with the Indians.
(e) That the recent fraudulent land grants be looked into.

The first brisk discussion arose over the declaration of causes. The convention was much divided as to whether there should be a declaration of fealty to the Mexican constitution of 1824, and a last final effort to maintain relations with the republic, or a declaration of independence.

John Austin Wharton, delegate from Brazoria, led the fight for an immediate declaration of independence, but Sam Houston and other older men urged a last stand for the federal constitution. Austin favored this course. There was a hope among the Texans even at this late hour, that there would be a faction in Mexico opposed to Santa Anna's usurpations, who would join Texas in a fight to preserve the constitution, and to this more than any other influence the convention yielded in the last sad effort to uphold the Mexican constitution after every Mexican state had succumbed.

Texas was soon undeceived in this vain hope, and when the next convention met in the following March, a declaration of independence was adopted at the opening hour and after that they proceeded to other business. In many respects the Consultation of 1835 was the most interesting convention which ever assembled in Texas. It was the third all-Texas convention that had met at San Felipe and the last, for the one in March met at Washington, on the Brazos.

A plan for a provisional government was made with great care and it provided for a Governor, a Lieutenant Governor and a General Council with a member from each municipality. The names of Henry Smith and Austin were placed before the convention for governor. Smith was chosen, for it was designed to send Austin as a commissioner to the United States. James W. Robinson, of Nacogdoches, was made lieutenant-governor. Article 14 of the Plan for Provisional Government closed the land office "during the unsettled and agitated condition of the country," so that no land grants could be made, and none were made until after the organization of the Republic in 1836.

Among the many worthy things done in this year, none speaks louder in the commendation of that generation of men than this precautionary act of closing the land office to protect the public domain.

The new government was without money or credit, and its land was the only possible source of revenue, and though they were in a death struggle and knew not where financial support was to be had, they placed the public domain in safekeeping for their children. How nobly they discharged this trust should ever be told to their praise.

Only a few years ago a wild scheme was proposed to found the Bank of Texas upon the credit of the school fund which came from this domain, but the hallowed memory of the fathers who kept it intact in the dark hours of the Revolution frustrated the design.

Stephen F. Austin, William H. Wharton and Dr. Branch T. Archer were chosen commissioners to the United States and urged to proceed there at once and use every means to arouse sympathy and procure assistance in the States.

The convention adjourned on November 14th, but issued a call for another to meet at Washington, on the Brazos, on March 1, 1836. The difficulties which confronted the new government are aptly stated in a single sentence of Governor Smith's first message to the Council on November 16th:

We have to call system out of chaos, to start the wheels of governments clogged by discordant interests. Without funds, without munitions of war, with an army in the field contending against a powerful foe, these are the auspices under which we are forced to make a beginning.

In the meantime while the consultation deliberated and the General Council sat, the Federal Army, as General Austin called it, was investing Bexar.

THE SIEGE OF BEXAR

The patriot army reached the suburbs of San Antonio in the last days of October, 1835. There were at that time about seven hundred men in the command. Austin divided them in two divisions, one of which was stationed below the city in the command of James Bowie, the other up the river under Edward Burleson.

There was much division of opinion as to whether the city should be stormed, and one studying the military tactics of the campaign is impressed with the entire want of discipline or vigorous command. Austin's health was bad and he had no military experience. While he was neither lacking in courage or firmness, yet he was by no means an ideal commander. Then, too, the volunteer army was an impromptu affair. Many of the men had left their families on exposed frontiers and would go home the first opportunity. The whole army was in a fair way to have disbanded and gone home, but was much encouraged by the arrival of the New Orleans Grays on November 21st. Though there were only sixty-four men in the company, yet it was the first installment of the effective help which came from the States to take part in the Revolution. Their arrival marks such an important and interesting chapter in our affairs that I feel justified in copying a page from the interesting history of John Henry Brown describing the event:

Late in the afternoon of November 21st, the New Orleans Grays, afterwards so distinguished for gallantry, the first to join the standard of Texas from the United States, arrived in the vicinity, and on the

22nd, reported themselves for duty. They numbered sixty-four men and had sailed from New Orleans in October on the schooner *Columbus* for the mouth of the Brazos with a supply of provisions and military stores contributed by the people of New Orleans. They were received with great enthusiasm at Velasco and Quintana, where ladies waved their handkerchiefs and men fired artillery. At Brazoria they were received with a yet more intense enthusiasm—flowers were strewn along their line of march and they were entertained there by Mrs. Jane H. Long, widow of General Long, often called the Mother of Texas. From Brazoria they marched on foot all of the way to San Antonio, stopping for a day at Victoria. Of all the companies which come out from the States, they stand out, preeminently. Many of them were murdered with Fannin's men four months later.

On November 24th, Austin and William H. Wharton left the army to accept the mission to the United States to which they had been chosen by the consultation a few days before. The army balloted for a commander-in-chief to take Austin's place, and Colonel Edward Burleson was chosen. Burleson was not a great commander, but he was a great fighter, and was long identified with Texas, and a glimpse of his eventful life will be interesting to this generation, for the name of Burleson has been an honored one in Texas history. He was born in North Carolina in 1798 and lived on the frontier all his long life. His grandfather and an uncle were killed by Indians in Eastern Tennessee, and an aunt was shot, tomahawked and scalped in the Wild West where the City of Nashville now stands.

The following interesting episode is told of him by his kinsman, the late Dr. Rufus C. Burleson:

When Edward was fourteen years old, he accompanied his father on an expedition into Alabama in pursuit of a roving band of Cherokees. The party was commanded by Jonathan Burleson, his uncle. The Indians planned to deceive their pursuers into a pow wow and massacre them, and each warrior concealed a knife under his garments ready for this wholesale homicide. As Burleson's men approached, they were met by an Indian warrior with an invitation to drink, which was the highest hospitality. The Captain reached out to take the proffered hand, when the Indian, quick as a flash, drew his knife and made a lunge at Captain Burleson, who sprang away and escaped injury. The Indian and the white man stood face to face, but the troopers could not fire for fear of hitting their Captain. It was a tragic moment when an instant meant eternity for some one. The boy was quicker to think and act than any of them and sprang forward firing as he did so and the Indian lay dead. The lad accompanied his father through the Tecumseh wars and was at the battle of Horseshoe Bend, where Houston won a wound which he carried all his life.

In 1826 he came to Texas and settled on the Colorado just below Bastrop, which for thirty years was the most dangerous of Texas frontiers.

He was at the Battle of San Jacinto, and lived for many years after these stirring days, and served one term as vice-president of the Republic. Dr. Rufus C. Burleson was at his deathbed when the old frontiersman had his summons, and relates his last conversation:

My life has been a rude one, and I have been a man of blood from my boyhood, but I have never fought for revenge. I have been in thirty-two battles but have lived to this old age and go now to meet my Maker.

Burleson was chosen commander on the 14th of November, and on the 4th of December an attack was begun which resulted in the capture of San Antonio after three days assault. But the world will always give the chief credit for this victory to Ben Milam, who lead the attack and fell in the fight.

BEN MILAM AND THE FALL OF BEXAR

It may be an exaggeration to ascribe to a single man the victory won by thousands, but we have come to link the name of the successful commander or bold leader with the battle won so that their names become synonyms.

Houston has so thoroughly monopolized the fame of San Jacinto that for years while he was in the United States Senate he was called "Old Sam Jacinto."

And so it will be, as long as the story of our colonial days is told, that Ben Milam will be known as the hero of the Battle of Bexar. He was a man of wonderful personality, taller than his fellows, powerful in mould and as handsome as one of Arthur's fabled knights.

On December 4, 1835, he returned from a successful scouting expedition towards the Rio Grande, and found much indecision as to whether the city should be stormed or the siege continued.

He walked among his countrymen and heard their quibbling and how some would fight, and others would wait and go home and renew the campaign in the spring, and without a council of war he made the bold defiance, *"Who will go into San Antonio with Old Ben Milam?"* And having thus advertised the excursion, he was quick to capitalize the enthusiasm it produced, and that very day the battle began which raged for six days and resulted in the capitulation of the Mexican army,

On the third day Milam was killed, and was buried where he fell. And now, thousands pass each day along the busy street of the city just off which stands the soldier's sepulcher.

And as we go on in this narrative and leave behind us the ashes of our hero dead, I cannot refrain from relating something of the life of Milam, for we shall not meet him again in these pages.

He was born in Kentucky in 1791, a year older than Austin and two years older than Houston. He was a soldier in the war of 1812, and as early as 1817 he and David G. Burnet were alone among the Comanches out on the headwaters of the Brazos. In 1819 he joined General Long and Felix Trespelacios in the ill-fated Long's Expedition into Texas. He was in Mexico at the close of the war for independence, and was among the first to apply for an empresario contract, but had to await the organization of the state government and got his grant in 1825 (along Red River). In an effort to finance his project, he went to England in 1827. A nephew of his who was a very small boy at that time and who lived to be a very old man, once told me the story of Milam's romance. He had a sweetheart when he left for England and she was to await his return. But when he was away another frontiersman rode that way and persuaded her to break her vows with the absent lover. She had some grounds for apprehension, for Ben was such a rover, and she did not know but that the next news of him might be that he had embarked in some enterprise on the other side of the world, or had gone to war with the Turks.

When Milam returned to his Red River colony, he brought with him silks and laces and much feminine finery he had bought for his bride, and this nephew told me how his Uncle Ben gave all these treasures to his (the lad's) mother, and took another journey down into Mexico.

In 1835 he was again among his colonists on the Red River. In those days there was much confusion caused by the Eleven Leaguers who were abroad in the land locating eleven league grants which were being handed out by the Coahuila government, and which often conflicted with the earlier empresario grants.

Milam undertook his last trip into Mexico in an effort to settle these tangled affairs, and left Red River with a few cold biscuits and some parched coffee to ride to the City of Mexico. He was at Monclova when the state government collapsed in 1835.

I cannot better close this narrative of Milam than by a literal quotation from the address of William H. Wharton delivered at the Hall of the Academy of Music in New York City on April 26, 1836. Wharton, with Austin and Archer, had gone as commissioners to the United States in the preceding December. They had gone through many of the states rousing sympathy and urging assistance for Texas. They made addresses in the leading cities. Two of these have come down to us and are classics of the period of the Revolution. One is the address of Austin made at Louisville, Kentucky, in February; the other Colonel Wharton's New York speech just referred to, and indeed it is the great masterpiece of our colonial history. The hall was crowded with an audience of thousands, for interest in Texas was very great everywhere in the states. News of the fall of the Alamo and the massacre of Goliad had reached the East and had been published in the daily papers. At the time this address was delivered, only the most awful information from Texas had reached the outside world, though the battle of San Jacinto had been fought five days before. But neither Wharton nor his hearers knew this, and they hourly expected news of even greater disaster than the Alamo or Goliad.

Wharton sought to arouse his great audience and all who would read his address to active support for Texas, for he knew that his people were in the death struggle, and he knew of no more stirring story than that of the last days of Ben Milam.

Here is his narrative: Governor Viesca of Coahuila was overtaken by Cos and imprisoned. It was the misfortune of the lamented Milam, who was returning from Mexico City to his home in Texas, to be found in company with the Governor. For this dreadful offence, he too was put in prison.

After some months imprisonment, he escaped and started for Texas. In order to elude pursuit, he traveled six hundred miles without a road, prosecuting his journey by night and secreting himself during the day.

Throughout this dangerous and protracted journey, he subsisted on some few articles of food which he had contrived to obtain on his escape from prison, for he dared not show his face at any habitation. Early in October he had gotten into Texas, and as he limped along the road he heard the approach of soldiers, and thinking he was about to be overtaken by his enemies, he hid himself by the road side. To his great joy he heard them talking his own tongue, and saw a company of Texas volunteers sweeping on their way to Goliad. He made himself known to them and went with them to Goliad and Gonzales. Though he had been an officer in the Army of the United States and a soldier in the war of 1812, he joined the ranks as a private and went on with the patriot army to San Antonio. On the evening of December 4th, he stepped from the ranks and beat up for volunteers to storm the Castle of San Antonio, and began an attack against heavy odds.

> *They entered the town to conquer or die,*
> *Firm paced and slow, a fearless front they formed,*
> *Still as the breeze, but dreadful as the storm.*

For six successive days and nights, they grappled with the foe, but the life of their leader was the price of their victory.

> *Oft shall the soldier think of thee,*
> *Thou dauntless leader of the brave,*
> *Who on the heights of tyranny,*
> *Won freedom—and a glorious grave.*
>
> *And o'er thy tomb shall pilgrims weep,*
> *And utter prayers in murmurs low,*
> *That peaceful be the Hero's sleep,*
> *Who conquered San Antonio.*
> *Enshrined on honor's deathless scroll,*
> *A nation's thanks shall be thy fame,*

Long as her beauteous rivers roll,
Shall Freedom's votaries hymn thy name.

This simple but beautiful poem dedicated to Milam had been published in a New York paper a few weeks before. The surrender of Cos' army left Texas free from Mexican soldiers. They were paroled and sent south. It was now December, but in a few short weeks they came again, Cos, with Santa Anna, Sesma, Filisola and Almonte, for now we are at the threshold of *Eighteen Hundred and Thirty-six.*

SAM HOUSTON

Houston will ever be the outstanding name in Texas history. It would be useless to attempt to have it otherwise, though the student of our annals should reach a different verdict as to the merit of the men who wrought in the scheme of our destiny. His tragic appearance into our affairs and the critical hour of his coming, the great success of the campaign of 1836, his long and eventful career, which only ended with secession, which he bitterly opposed a quarter of a century later—add to all these a stern, sterling character and a personality rarely found among the heroes of any age, and one will not wonder why Sam Houston has become by universal consent the hero of our history. He was an actor of great skill, a spectacular man wholly unlike the modest, reticent Austin. When Houston came, Austin was dying. Fourteen years of privation, labor without ceasing, days and nights on horseback across trackless wilds, had written deep traces in the sad, white face which William J. Russell saw in the flickering candlelight that October night at Gonzales. Houston came with the flush of victory in 1836, and December of that year Austin died.

In 1832, when the first rumblings of the coming Revolution were heard, Houston, who was yet under forty, was living among the Cherokee Indians in Arkansas.

He had resigned the governorship of Tennessee and sought this voluntary exile three years before, and during all this retirement he is known to have entertained thoughts of coming to Texas. Wild rumors of his intentions to lead the Cherokees in an attack upon Mexican authority in Texas assumed such proportions as to cause President Jackson, always his devoted friend, to write him a personal letter of remonstrance. There has been and will be much speculation as to whether there was any understanding between Houston and Jackson which preceded Houston's coming.

While many circumstances would suggest this, yet I do not believe it existed. That they both hoped for just such a result as obtained, is but natural.

Franklin Williams, grandson of General Houston, has the original passport issued to Houston for his first journey into Texas, which was then a foreign country, in 1832. The document has never before been published as far as I know.

SAM HOUSTON PASSPORT

I, the undersigned, Acting Secretary of War, do hereby request all the Tribes of Indians, whether in amity with the United States, or as yet not allied to them by Treaties, to permit safely and freely to pass through their respective Territories,

—General Sam Houston—

a citizen of the United States, thirty-eight years of age, six feet two inches in stature, brown hair, and light complexion; and in case of need, to give him all lawful aid and protection.

(SEAL) GIVEN UNDER my hand and the impression of the SEAL of the DEPARTMENT OF WAR, at the City of Washington, this Sixth day of August, in the Year of OUR LORD One Thousand eight hundred and thirty-two, and of the Independence of the UNITED STATES, the fifty seventh.

(Signed) JOHN ROBB,
Acting Secretary of War

Armed with this passport, he came from Arkansas via Nacogdoches and San Felipe to San Antonio in December, 1832, where he had a conference with the Mexican authorities and with a delegation of Comanche Indians, who were sometimes roving residents of the States. I have never been able to find any tangible reason for this strange visit of Houston under a commission from the American Secretary of War. Upon his return to Natchitoches, Louisiana, in January, 1833, he wrote President Jackson, advising, "Having been as far as Bexar in the Province of Texas, I had an interview with the Comanche Indians; I am in possession of information which will be of interest to you and may be calculated to forward your views if you should entertain any touching the acquisition of Texas, etc."

The entire letter is devoted to a discussion of Texas' internal affairs and the anxiety of the Americans in Texas for union with the States, with a mere mention of the ostensible mission which had taken him to Texas. He advised that a convention would be held in Texas in April, and "I expect to be present and will advise you of the course adopted." He did attend the 1833 convention as a delegate from San Augustine. In 1834 he was back among the Cherokees in Arkansas, but late in that year he took up his residence at Nacogdoches, and we find him a delegate from that municipality to the consultation which convened at San Felipe in October, 1835.

Just before the consultation met, he rode down to the Guadalupe for a visit to the patriot army, then on its way to San Antonio. Noah Smithwick, who was with the army, tells of his arrival mounted on a yellow Spanish stud, and that he made a speech and rode back to the Brazos for the convention.

He was a strong person in the consultation; a man of rare experience in governmental matters, and looked upon as the confidential friend of the President of the United States. He had now definitely decided to cast his lot with Texas and aimed at leadership. On November 14th, the day before Edward Burleson was elected *viva voce* to command the army at Bexar, when Austin left for the United States, the General Council sitting in San Felipe selected Houston commander-in-chief of the Texas armies. But this high sounding phrase was a bitter mockery for Texas had no government, no war chest, no army.

After the fall of Bexar in December, the volunteers took leave for their homes, only a small garrison remaining. The months which followed were full of confusion and gloom. The General Council at San Felipe degenerated into a vicious quarrel, poor old Governor Smith writing philippic messages of denunciation, and a majority against him refusing to act upon any plan he would suggest. There were those in Texas who yet entertained the fond hope that a party in Mexico would rise to cooperate in resistance to Santa Anna, and there was considerable sentiment immediately following the success at Bexar for an invasion of Mexico.

James Fannin, whose martyrdom a few months later silenced criticism, was the chief in the proposed Mexican invasion. Instead of a concerted action for defense against the large Mexican army now known to be mustering for approach by way of San Antonio, Fannin and Dr. John Grant and others with authority from the General Council, and without cooperation with Houston, wasted the early months of 1836 and frustrated Houston's plans for an organized defense.

In the mad political strife of the late fifties, when Senator Houston would not go with the extreme secessionists and left the Democratic party, bitter attacks were made on him and much effort was made to show that he was a coward, that the battle of San Jacinto was won in spite of him, and volumes of invectives were written against him.

I have read all the evidences that are available and am persuaded that no case is made against the old hero. Those best able to judge him were his comrades in the 1836 campaign. The first presidential election was held within four months after the battle. By common consent he was nominated and elected to the presidency almost by acclamation, although both Austin and Henry Smith were his opponents. He was again chosen President of the Republic after Lamar's term; and when Texas was admitted to the Union he was chosen U. S. Senator almost without dissent, when the legislature which elected him was filled with men who went through the San Jacinto campaign.

And as the ages come and go, in remote years yet to be, when other names of the colonial epoch are forgotten, this strange, stalwart, tragic man will stand out not only the most interesting character in our history but one of the most remarkable men of all time.

Eighteen Hundred and Thirty-Six

This is the all-eventful year in Texas history.

The Declaration of Independence was made at Washington on the Brazos on March 2nd.

The Alamo fell on March 6th.

Fannin fell at Goliad March 27th.

San Jacinto was fought on April 21st.

The first presidential election was held and Houston elected President in September.

The first Congress of the Republic met at Columbia October 3rd.

Austin died December 27th.

The dawn of the year saw a small garrison of about 150 men at Bexar, and though it was known that a large Mexican army was being organized for invasion, there was no plan or concerted action for defense.

The quarrel between Governor Smith and the Council had reached the riot stage, and he had been deposed and James W. Robinson, of Nacogdoches, lieutenant governor, reigned in his stead. And in passing I must say a word about "Lawyer Robinson."

After the Council had ceased to function, when the convention met in March, he joined the army and was at the Battle of San Jacinto. He was one of the first District Judges under the Republic, and in 1842 was attending court at San Antonio when a Mexican marauding force under Woll, captured the city, court and all, and Judge Robinson found himself in a Mexican prison. Tiring of prison life, he opened an intrigue with Santa Anna, who happened to be in power again at that particular interval, and wrote the Mexican president a letter advising that since he (Robinson) was a lawyer of some prominence in his own country he might be useful if allowed his freedom in persuading the people of Texas to return to Mexican sovereignty. Santa Anna seemed impressed with the idea and allowed Lawyer Robinson, yet in prison, to open negotiations with President Houston, who was then serving his second term. Houston seems to have humored the joke, and Robinson got out of Mexico to complete his negotiations, which were dropped as soon as he got home.

Shortly after the discovery of gold in California in 1849, both Robinson and Henry Smith joined an emigrant train across the desert, and these veteran enemies traveled together in a wagon train for a thousand miles, each nursing his old-time hatred for the other. Judge Robinson's wife, Sarah, a beautiful and accomplished woman, who had come to Texas with him in 1828, went with him to California and was still living there fifty years later. They had gotten their headright league in Vehlein's Colony and after Robinson's death in California many years later, Sarah sold this league. About twenty years ago I represented one of the owners of this land in a suit brought by the descendants of James W. Robinson of Ohio. They alleged and proved that he had eloped from Ohio in 1827 with Sarah, leaving a wife and children, and these grandchildren came to claim their inheritance from their prodigal ancestor. Maybe this little bit of scandal should remain untold. But it is part of the judicial history of San

Jacinto County, where depositions were filed proving these facts.

At the beginning of 1836, Lieutenant Governor James W. Robinson dominated in general council. James Fannin and Dr. John Grant and Frank Johnson were planning an invasion of Mexico by Matamoros. They had fewer than 500 men, and were without means of transportation or supplies. General Houston was unable to exercise any authority, though he was in name commander-in-chief of the army. He bided the assembling of the convention, which was called to meet in March, and used the interval in a series of conversations with the Indians, whose attitude was a matter of much concern at this juncture. If the Comanches and Cherokees had gone on the warpath against the colonists early in 1836, the Americans would have been wiped out. All available men were being pressed to join the army to repel the Mexican invasion. Families were left unprotected on a wide frontier, which reached from San Antonio to the Sabine. There were bands of Indian warriors all along this frontier who could have swept over the settlements in a week. Houston went in person among these people and held thirteen councils with them. He was a Cherokee chief, and all his life loved and was loved by the Indians. To him we owe the fact that these warriors did not draw the bow during the campaign of 1836.

Franklin Williams, a grandson of General Houston, recently related in my hearing an account of a pow wow between Houston and the Indians which had been told him by his mother. A delegation of Cherokees came several days' journey to see him. They had ridden day and night for several days. They came within a few hundred yards of the house, and after hobbling their tired horses they sat in a circle under a tree, leaving an open or vacant space in the circle. They did not look towards the house or make any pretense of seeing Houston. Nor did he see them, but pretended to ignore them for a time. After a while he moved and occupied the vacant place in the circle, but no word was spoken, or glance of recognition given. The pipe was passed from hand to hand and they all puffed it.

And after a long dignified silence, their spokesman began the conversation and made known the purpose of their journey. The president heard their story, and promised them redress, and then he bade them kill a beef for their refreshment, for they had not eaten during the long journey in which they had ridden day and night, nor had they slept. After they had gorged the beef without the detail of cooking it, the entire delegation lay under the trees and slept for a day and a night, and then they silently mounted their horses and retraced their long way whence they came, riding without rest until they reached their people.

One cannot but wish that the white brother had something of this great gift of golden silence.

It would be hard indeed to picture a darker prospect than fronted our people at the dawn of the year 1836. The president of Mexico, with an army of almost ten thousand men, was moving towards the border. Fannin, Grant, Johnson and other visionary incompetents were trying to lead five hundred men to an invasion of Mexico. A mere handful of volunteers garrisoned the outpost at San Antonio.

The General Council, our governing body, had gone to pieces. There was not 1,000 men under arms in all Texas. Without a government, without an army, without a treasury, without credit, the colonies faced dire disaster at the dawn of 1836.

THE CONVENTION OF MARCH, 1836

For the fourth time in our history, a convention of all Texas met on March 1, 1836, at Washington on the Brazos. Without a moment's delay, a permanent organization was had with Richard Ellis, from Red River, as chairman.

The General Council was still in session at San Felipe, but its conspicuous failures earned it the contempt of the new convention. An effort was made to have the convention go into merits of the quarrel between Governor Smith and the Council, but the convention hurried to the tasks before it and declined to take any notice of the controversy, and the whole pitiful farce passed into history. It is fair to Governor Smith to say that that generation exonerated his fidelity and integrity, but probably not his judgment.

As soon as the convention was ready for business, George C. Childress, of the Red River country, moved the appointment of a committee of five to draft a declaration of independence. Tradition tells that he had already prepared the draft of the declaration and that it had been approved by Houston and others to whom it had been submitted. The committee brought in the draft the next morning, and when it was read on motion of General Houston, it was unanimously adopted early in the morning of March 2, 1836, which by the way was his 43rd birthday.

On the 4th Houston was again chosen commander-in chief, and on Sunday morning, March 6th, the same hour the Alamo fell, he left Washington with an escort of four men riding towards San Antonio. At that time it was known to Houston and to the convention that there was no hope for Travis, and that no help could be expected from Fannin and Grant and those mad, mislead men who had lately moved towards remote Matamoros while Santa Anna's army marched directly into the heart of Texas.

In a cold March rain, the five horsemen rode west while sad, sober faces bade them goodbye and turned to the business of the convention.

Speaking of this occasion, General Houston said many years later: "The only hope lay in the few men assembled at Gonzales. The Alamo was known to be under siege, Fannin was known to be embarrassed, Ward, Morris and Johnson destroyed. All seemed to bespeak a calamity of the most direful character. It was under these auspices that the General started with an escort of two aides, a captain and a boy, yet he was sent to produce a nation and defend a people."

Travis' last message, sent from the Alamo on March 3rd, reached Washington on Sunday morning, just before Houston left, and about the hour the Alamo fell, and was read in the convention at its opening session on that day, but there was nothing the convention could do except to adopt a resolution that *"1,000 copies of the letter be printed,"* and this they arranged for.

With independence declared and Houston on the way west, the convention addressed itself to the formation of our first constitution, for our fathers were firm believers in constitutional government. With them it was as natural for a new government to have a solemnly written constitution as for an infant to be christened and bear his father's name.

In these awful environments, the constitution of March, 1836, was written, debated and adopted, and prepared for submission to the people for ratification. But no man knew when if ever there could be a submission at a general election, and until this was done a government ad interim was provided. David G. Burnet was chosen president and the Mexican-Spaniard Lorenzo de Zavala, lately fled from Mexico to escape Santa Anna, was chosen vice-president.

The last hours of the convention, which finished its labors late on the night of March 17th, were hastened by a rumor that a Mexican army was near at hand. News of the fall of the Alamo had come by a courier on the 15th, but there was no unseemly haste on the part of the convention.

The constitution which was formulated by this convention was never formally enrolled or engrossed, and the original draft was taken away by H. S. Kimball, the secretary, who was instructed to enroll it for presentation. He took it to Nashville, Tennessee, where it was published in one of the papers, from which it was republished in a Cincinnati paper, and from this Cincinnati publication it was copied in the first issue of Borden's paper, which was printed after the Revolution at Columbia on August 2nd. Late in the afternoon of the last day, the president left for Harrisburg, and there was only one family left in Washington on the Brazos.

There are fifty-eight signers of the Declaration of Independence which this convention promulgated on March 2nd. Forty of them were under forty years of age. Many of them were men highly educated and of rare experience. Nearly all of them came from the southern states, eleven from the Carolinas. There were two native Texans, Jose Antonio Navarro and Francisco Ruis, both from Bexar. There was an Englishman, a Canadian, a Spaniard born in Madrid, an Irishman and a Scotchman.

The leaders in Texas during all these years were for the most part slave-holding planters, and though that oft-called slave-holding oligarchy paid the extreme penalty in the next generation, yet its aggressiveness and love of dominion and empire won Texas and the great southwest for the American Union.

The Alamo

At the beginning of the Revolution and for many years theretofore, an old Spanish mission fortress stood on the San Antonio River about a mile from the center of the little city. It derived its name from the cottonwood trees which grew about it. Adjoining the chapel was a stone walled enclosure of about two city blocks, which had been erected as a protection against the Indians. After the patriot army had captured the city in December, 1835, many of the volunteer soldiers had gone home, and those remaining were disorganized and without supplies.

Colonel Neill remained nominally in charge of the garrison quartered in the Alamo, which, on January 14th, consisted of eighty-six men.

Immediately following the fall of the city to the Texas army, the wild scheme was advanced for the invasion of Mexico by Matamoros, and Frank W. Johnson, and the ill-fated Scotchman, Dr. John Grant, persuaded a large number to join them in this fool's enterprise, and they forgathered at Goliad, San Patricio, and other places in that direction.

All Texas knew at the dawn of 1836 that a large Mexican army was being formed to march upon Texas, and almost daily rumors and confirmed reports came that these armies were approaching the Rio Grande. In the face of this deadly disaster, a sad state of affairs presented itself.

Governor Smith wrote letters and sent couriers and did his utmost to get reinforcements to the Alamo, but the council deposed him and commissioned Fannin, Grant, and Johnson to invade Mexico, though there were not 500 men in sight for such an enterprise. Houston, commander-in-chief, had no army to command nor prospect of any. He advised that the garrison at the Alamo destroy the fortress and retreat east of the Guadalupe, but his advice was ignored. He urged Fannin, who with several hundred men was near Goliad, to retreat to Victoria, but Fannin refused to recognize his authority. In January, Governor Smith sent Colonel Travis, who was recruiting on the Colorado, to relieve Colonel Neill in command at the Alamo, and in this way conferred on this young officer the boon of martyrdom and immortality. In February, as the Mexican army approached, Travis and James Bowie, who was now with him, began sending out couriers begging frantically for help, but always declaring that whether relief came they would defend to the last.

As late as February 12th, after Travis knew Santa Anna's army was approaching, he wrote Governor Smith, "With two hundred men I believe this place can be maintained."

On February 23rd, Travis reported the enemy in sight, and on that day a large army camped on the main plaza, a mile away, and the siege began and continued in a desultory way for ten days, during which time a bombardment was kept up, and the Mexican forces entirely surrounded the beleaguered fortress.

In the early morning of March 1st, Captain Albert Martin with thirty-one men came through the Mexican lines from Gonzales, and took their places with the defenders, and near noon on March 3rd, the gallant James B. Bonham, who had been sent as a messenger to Fannin, rode back through the enemy lines to report no aid from that source. So that there were something more than one hundred and eighty men in the command at the end. Almost the same hour that Bonham came, Travis sent John Smith with the last of his series of bold messages, which reached the colonies only after the Alamo had fallen.

A council of war was held on March 4th, at which the Mexican command decided to storm the fortress at dawn on Sunday morning, March 6th. General Castrillon was put in command of the immediate assault. The silence of the early dawn was broken by a shrill bugle blast which summoned the charge, and as the tramp of the on-rushing troops filled the March morning, a band from a nearby battery struck up a Spanish air which was known as the assassin's song, and meant no mercy. In sight of the besieged men, a black flag floated from a steeple. Less than an hour elapsed from the first assault until the last defender had fallen.

Castrillon led the assault, and Santa Anna remained with a battery from Toluca camped to the south and safe from gunshot, where the band played the assassin's song while the assault went on.

On the same day and after the fort had fallen, he made an official report to the Secretary of War from which I take some interesting passages:

The scene offered by the engagement was extraordinary. Twenty-one pieces of artillery was used with most perfect accuracy and illuminated the interior of the fortress. The fortress is now in our power and the corpses of more than six hundred foreigners were buried in the ditches. A great many who escaped the bayonet of the infantry, fell under the sabres of the cavalry. I can assure your Excellency that few are those who bore their associates the tidings of the disaster. Among the corpses are those of Bowie and Travis, who styled themselves Colonels, and also that of Crockett. Nor will we hereafter suffer any foreigners, whatever their origin may be, to pollute our soil. I shall in due time send your Excellency a circumstantial report of this glorious triumph.

It is not related whether the band with the Toluca Battery continued to play the assassin's song while his Excellency wrote this report, but one would surmise so as the strains of that song and sentiment abound in his diction.

We first meet and part with Crockett at the Alamo. He had only come to Texas a few weeks before from Tennessee. He had been a member of Congress from Tennessee two terms and had gained a national reputation as a whig and opponent of President Jackson, who came from his own state. In the recent elections he had been defeated and in his characteristic style said his constituents could go to hell and he would go to Texas. He was a stalwart, picturesque frontiersman, and those who have looked upon his portrait as it hangs in the entrance to our State House at Austin can but be impressed that he was a splendid specimen of frontier manhood.

The outstanding feature of this great tragedy was the grim determination of the defenders to sell their lives in what they knew was a futile effort to hold the fort. Travis and his followers could have escaped to Gonzales and retreated with Houston, but this fact, though obvious to them, was never given a serious thought. They were determined to die in the Alamo at the threshold of Texas.

But the nearly two weeks they delayed the advance of the Mexican army was as valuable to Texas as the sacrifice of Belgium in the path of the Kaiser's armies which saved Paris. It allowed the settlers between the Guadalupe and the Brazos time to escape. While the Alamo was falling the convention at Washington was forming a government to take place of the poor, miserable General Council.

And as night fell on San Antonio on that beautiful March day, the roar of battle and the sounds of the assassin's song died away, and the mangled forms of our dead were piled like debris in the shadow of the old Mission.

The invading army, over seven thousand men, waited orders to march on east and exterminate the "foreigners who were polluting the soil."

GOLIAD

The most terrible atrocity of the Revolution was the massacre at Goliad. One who studies this awful tragedy after the lapse of years is alternately moved with pity and contempt for poor Fannin. If his blunders had cost him only his life we could well forget his stubborn stupidity. He had a little West Point training, and is a conspicuous example of the very old truth that "a little learning is a dangerous thing."

But the blood of those who fell with Fannin may well be upon the heads of the Council at San Felipe which deposed Gov. Smith and loaned the semblance of authority to an invasion of Mexico by way of Matamoros. Or, as Fannin put it, "carry the war into Mexico to keep it out of Texas."

After the capture of San Antonio in December, Fannin, who was with the army, visited San Felipe and succeeded in getting a commission from the General Council which authorized him to concentrate forces at Copano, a port on

Aransas Bay, and in January he issued a call to volunteers to join him in such an enterprise. Just at this time Major William Ward, with the Georgia Battalion, arrived at Velasco, and Fannin being a Georgian and known to many of them, they hastened to join him. In the meantime Dr. John Grant, who was with the army at Bexar, conceived the idea that he would lead an invasion into Mexico on his own account, and not desiring to march with Fannin, he got permission from the Council and moved to Goliad with fewer than two hundred men bent on carrying the war into Mexico.

Several hundred volunteers had arrived at the mouth of the Brazos since the opening of hostilities, and they were being diverted to Copano and other places towards the southwest for this enterprise. All supplies and munitions which were being shipped by sea for the patriot army were being landed at points along the Gulf, and for the most part, they were being taken over by Fannin or concentrated for use in his campaign.

The small garrison at the Alamo remained isolated while Johnson, Grant and Fannin rushed their mad schemes for a descent upon Matamoros. In January, General Houston, who had been named commander-in-chief by the General Council in the previous November, went down to Goliad and San Patricio in an effort to organize these wild, discordant elements, but nearly every man he met had a commission from the General Council at San Felipe to act independently, and none of them would act with the others or with Houston.

He returned therefore to await the action of the convention, which was to assemble in March. But the invading army would not await the action of the convention. Santa Anna was early advised of the purpose of the Texans to attack Matamoros, and sent General Urrea there with a substantial force, and while the main army marched from Laredo towards San Antonio, Urrea, with probably 1,500 men, came into Texas from Matamoros. On

February 27th, only three days after the Mexican army reached San Antonio and began the siege of the Alamo, the advance guard of Urrea's division reached San Patricio, where they attacked Frank W. Johnson's small command, who were scouting about the country in an aimless fashion. Johnson was one of the commanders commissioned by the unhappy council at San Felipe to lead an invasion into Mexico. All of Johnson's men were killed except himself and four others who escaped. Urrea's men next located Dr. John Grant and his men.

On March 2nd, the very day the convention at Washington declared independence, Grant's command was attacked about twenty miles from San Patricio, and all but one were killed or captured. Urrea reported forty-one killed and six prisoners.

A story has long been told in Texas that the Mexicans bound Dr. Grant to a wild mustang, and that he was dashed to death in that fashion. The surviving witness tells that he saw Grant fall and several Mexican soldiers running their swords through his body. Grant was a Scotchman, but had lived long years in Mexico, and they seemed to have a particular enmity towards him. These commanders, Johnson and Grant, had been styled the advance division of the volunteer army for the invasion of Mexico, and their early annihilation was a sad blow to Fannin's men at Goliad.

On March 10th, Fannin sent Captain King with twenty-eight men to relieve some families at Refugio, and hearing two days later that King's men were surrounded in the mission there, he sent Colonel Ward with his one hundred and fifty Georgia volunteers to aid King. King's command was destroyed and about one hundred of Ward's men succeeded in retreating to Victoria, where they were captured on March 22nd, and sent back to Goliad to be shot with Fannin's men.

After making many plans and abandoning them all, poor Fannin attempted at the last hour to retreat from

Goliad, and succeeded in getting some miles when they halted in an open prairie, in a depression away from shelter or water, and were surrounded by Mexicans and attacked on all sides.

Here the battle of Coleto was fought, where the Texans defended themselves with great bravery, but without ammunition or artillery, they were soon at the mercy of Urrea's men, and a parley was opened for their surrender. On March 20th they surrendered, the terms being:

1. That they surrender at discretion.
2. That the wounded and their commander Fannin be treated with all consideration possible.
3. That the whole detachment be treated as prisoners at the disposal of the Supreme Government.

They were removed to Goliad, where they were held in captivity along with a command of men from Nashville, Tennessee, under Colonel Miller, who had been captured as they landed at Copano.

Urrea, who had gone to Victoria, left orders that the prisoners be treated humanely, but His Excellency remembered that the Supreme Government had passed a decree that all foreigners taken in arms should be executed as pirates, and under his orders the entire command were marched out at dawn on March 27th, and shot to death.

The gruesome details of this massacre have so often been told that they need not be repeated here. About twenty of them were spared, most of whom were physicians and who were thought of some possible use. Thirty-four escaped in various ways—three hundred and sixty-four fell.

J. C. Duval, who escaped by dashing away as they fired, wrote a very interesting account of it in later years, and relates that among the prisoners in the Kentucky Company to which he belonged, was a young man who had been a roommate at college in Kentucky with a Mexican officer in Urrea's command, that these young men found each other and the Mexican officer professed sympathy and kindness for his former boyhood friend, but made not the slightest effort to assist him or save him, and saw him shot to death without any apparent concern.

THE RUNAWAY SCRAPE

The colonists returning to their homes after the battle in April always spoke lightly of the retreat as the "Runaway Scrape."

An eyewitness who was in Gonzales on the evening of the eighth of March tells of the terror which was inspired by the news of the butchery at the Alamo. Many of the victims were from DeWitt's Colony, and the twilight was filled with the screams of women and fatherless children bereft by that disaster. When General Houston reached Gonzales on March 11th, he found three hundred and seventy-four men half fed, half clad, half armed and unorganized. Every wagon available but one was employed in moving the women and children, for all Texas began to move eastward. One wagon with four oxen was devoted to the removal of the munitions of war, and it was not overloaded.

As the retreat from Gonzales proceeded, one hundred and twenty-five reinforcements came up at Peach Creek, but news of the Alamo caused twenty-five of them to desert the same night.

When the retreat reached the Colorado, there were five hundred men with Houston, but they had no artillery, not a cartridge or a ball. When they reached Nevada Creek they heard that a blind mother with six children had been left some miles below and a detachment was sent to bring her away.

The "army" halted at the Colorado until all fugitives had crossed. On the Colorado news came of Fannin's fall at Goliad, and a detachment of the Mexican army under

Sesma came in sight on the western bank of the river. There was an expectation that certain ordnance from the mouth of the Brazos would reach the camp at the Colorado. Without it Houston dared not risk a battle, and we now know that a battle with Sesma would have decided nothing. The army as well as the whole population of Texas fell back to the Brazos. The men with Houston were in a bad humor. He had taken no one into his confidence, and in fact never did do so until the very last. At times it seemed as though there would be open mutiny and that the whole command would go to pieces, and this would no doubt have resulted but for the constant pressure of the invading army, which now approached San Felipe. In fact there was very little command, and heavy April rains retarded both armies. Houston effected a crossing of the Brazos some miles north of San Felipe, but the Mexican army could not follow for the awful condition of the ground and dropped down to Richmond, where an advance guard under Santa Anna crossed.

There have come down to us some graphic pictures of those days which intervened between the fall of the Alamo and San Jacinto. In the first volume of the Texas Historical Quarterly, Mrs. Rosa Kleberg, who was, at the time she related the incidents, eighty-five years old, tells a story which will fairly illustrate the plight and flight of all Texas. Her husband and brothers joined the army, and the women in the family, with the father, migrated towards the east.

Most of the families traveled separately until they reached the Brazos, where all were compelled to halt for a crossing. I helped drive the cattle and carried my infant daughter in the saddle before me. When the families and their horses and cattle reached the crossing, the noise was terrible. There was only one small ferry boat, which would carry one vehicle at a time. Deaf Smith's Mexican wife was in a truck wheeled cart, a cart with two wooden wheels made from an entire cross section of a large tree, with her two pairs of twins, but had no team to pull her cart. My brother carried her for a distance with his yoke of oxen. The next day after we crossed over the Brazos, we camped near Clear Creek, where Louis V. Reader, my brother's child, was born in a corn crib.

The government ad interim, which was organized at Washington on the Brazos left for Harrisburg, hurried by the report that Sesma's army was approaching. President Burnet sent back hurried messages to Houston to stop his retreat and fight, but continued to retreat until he reached Galveston Island. And indeed he only escaped by a hair's breadth, for as he pulled off from Lynchburg in a skiff, Mexican soldiers were in sight and hastened his voyage with some target practice.

Gail and Thomas H. Borden published a paper at San Felipe known as the *Texas Telegraph & Register*. It played a conspicuous part in those troubled days. As the Mexican army approached San Felipe, the town was deserted and destroyed, and the Borden printing business, loaded on an ox-wagon, started across the water logged prairie for Harrisburg, following the fugitive footsteps of the fleeing government ad interim.

On April 14th, it was temporarily housed at Harrisburg, and as there was no hostile army in sight, the plucky publishers, delayed by this removal, started their weekly paper with an apology for the delay and the reassuring salutation, "Our subscribers on hearing the ruin of San Felipe and seeing the delay in the appearance of our paper, have perhaps thought it at an end."

After recounting the difficulties in the way and the great need of a newspaper just at this time the weekly publication under date of April 14th, was begun. It recounts the doleful news that the Mexicans had scoured the country as far as the Brazos, with an army at San Felipe, and one at Brazoria, while the central division had crossed at Richmond. Just here the April 14th edition of the paper stops, for at this point advance scouting parties of Santa Anna's army were reported near Harrisburg, and Borden took a few copies of so much of the paper as had been struck off and moved on. There are a half dozen or more copies of this half-finished edition of April 14th yet in existence. His press was destroyed, and I have it from the Borden family that they threw it in the Bayou to prevent its falling into Mexican hands.

There was a further suspension of the publication from April 14th, but on August 2nd, these same indomitable Bordens published the next issue at Columbia, where the government ad interim was then sojourning and the next year they followed the new government to Houston, where the paper was published for many years.

All Texas was now east of the Brazos. The Mexican army had been divided into divisions, which swept the country north as far as the San Antonio-Nacogdoches Road, south along the coast, while His Excellency with what he called the "flower of the army" hurried along in advance and crossed the Brazos at Fort Bend, and pushed on after the fleeing provisional government.

The only armed force which the Texans had, if indeed it could be called such, was the disorganized, unhappy, forlorn few hundred with Houston, who were pulling across the muddy prairies from San Felipe.

General Houston, grim and silent, seemed heading for the Red Lands, and thousands of fleeing families hurried their weary way on across the Trinity. These fugitives returned home in April, after the battle, and most of them planted a crop and reaped a harvest in that year.

San Jacinto

After the fall of the Alamo, Santa Anna planned to return to Mexico and leave the minor incidents of the further campaign to Filisola, but was dissuaded by Almonte, and decided to come on further east. He sent Sesma's division after Houston's retreating army on the Colorado, with instructions to march via San Felipe and Harrisburg to Anahuac, where they would be embarked for home by sea. He sent Gaona direct to Nacogdoches. He did not seem to contemplate any serious opposition anywhere.

Colonel Morales, with four companies, were sent to Goliad to join Urrea's army, which had come into Texas by Matamoros, and which was then engaged with. Fannin, Grant, Johnson and King. His Excellency left Bexar for San Felipe March 29th, where he arrived on April 7th. Houston's little army had abandoned San Felipe a week before, going up the river to Groce's. The Mexicans would have followed but for high water. The Brazos bottom was as kind as the Red Sea, in that it allowed Houston's army to retreat but was impassable for the invading army to follow. Santa Anna, unable to follow or cross the river at San Felipe, moved down to Richmond. Houston crossed at Groce's on the 13th, and took up his march across the wet roadless prairie almost south towards Harrisburg. On the 14th, Santa Anna crossed the Brazos at Richmond, riding hard with six hundred picked men for Harrisburg, where he hoped to capture President Burnet and the government ad interim.

He was in great good humor, and as they crossed Oyster Creek near where Sugarland now stands, he enjoyed the noise and confusion that the cavalry made as it floundered in the "Muddy Squishy Creek." As the mules and muleteers floundered in the mire and the drivers swore as mule drivers have always done, His Excellency sat on his horse and laughed as though it was all improvised for his amusement.

One cannot overlook the contrast in these two armies as they converged across the prairies. His Excellency, flushed with victory, rode with a shining staff accompanied by such men as Almonte and Castrillon. It was a kind of holiday excursion for him, for this was his first (and last) visit to Texas. The little Texas army, if in fact it can be called such, consisted of fewer than 1,000 tired, hungry men, many of whom had not eaten an adequate meal for weeks. On the night before they crossed the bayou, Houston slept on the ground in his wet clothes, with a saddle for a pillow, while a keen April norther added to the discomfort.

The Mexicans reached Harrisburg on the night of the 15th, and left the next day to scour the country down to the bay, intending to cross the bayou and the river above their confluence and go on to Nacogdoches or Anahuac. Santa Anna sent Houston word by a negro that as soon as he cleaned out the land thieves, meaning the government officials, and probably the people east of the Trinity, he would pay his respects to Houston.

A more foolhardy plan than Santa Anna had devised could not well be imagined. He had come into Texas with more than seven thousand five hundred men, and the morning of the sixteenth when he rode out to Harrisburg going down to the bay with only about six hundred men, his forces were scattered in small divisions all the way to Bexar.

Urrea was coming along the coast from Goliad with one thousand five hundred men. Gaona was near La Grange with seven hundred and fifty. Sesma was on the Brazos at Fort Bend with one thousand. Filisola, with nearly two thousand, was coming down the river from San Felipe seeking a crossing. Cos with five hundred was trying to keep up with the mad fool who with his fleetest cavalry was dashing across the prairie after the government.

Houston learned definitely on the 18th that the advance force had passed Harrisburg, and that Santa Anna was with it, and the Texas army crossed from the north side of the bayou on the 19th and pushed on down to the confluence of the bayou with the San Jacinto River, where it camped.

This point was chosen to prevent Santa Anna from crossing further up.

It has been charged that General Houston never in tended to fight; that he expected to continue his retreat to the Red Lands with the hope of getting help from the troops under General Gaines of the United States army, who were camped at the border, and many of whom were eager to get into this fight. It is evident that Houston hoped for help from East Texas which never came. Just before crossing the bayou for the purpose of going after Santa Anna, he wrote a letter to Henry Rouget of the Committee of Safety at Nacogdoches, deploring the fact that no help had come from the Red Lands and announcing that he was now about to cross the bayou for the purpose of attacking Santa Anna's army. It has been charged that the battleground was selected by accident, and the most disadvantageous point that could have been found along the bayou. This is not true. In the first place it is high ground on the banks of the river. Then again it was in the edge of a woods which gave a commanding view of the prairies across which it was necessary for the Mexican army to approach.

On the morning of April 20, that portion of Santa Anna's army which had been scouring the bay shore, turned back toward the bayou and came in sight of the Texas army camping in the woods, which can be seen probably a mile away from the monuments on what we call the battleground.

On the morning of the 21st, Cos with his detachment of something more than five hundred men, joined the command, swelling the Mexican forces to something over one thousand five hundred men. There was much complaint and criticism among Houston's men and no little distrust of him had arisen among his under officers. From the time he left Gonzales until this hour, he had communicated his designs to no one, and his silence gave weight to the thought that he had no defined plans and that he did not intend to fight. He held a council of war with his under-officers on the forenoon of the 21st, in which it was warmly debated whether they should attack the enemy or await the enemy's attack. It was urged that the Mexican army was composed of veteran soldiers, and it was known that very few of the Texans had ever seen other than Indian warfare. Houston got the ideas of those present, but did not express himself at this council meeting. It was nearly 4 o'clock on the afternoon of the 21st before he finally gave the order to Colonel John A. Wharton, the Judge Advocate General, and instructed him to form the army for an immediate offensive. If this order had not been given at 4 o'clock, there would have been a mutiny before sundown. The army and its leaders were on the point of forcing the issue. The excitement was intense, and if indeed the grim old Cherokee chief had a design to work his men up to a point of frenzy for a fight, he managed it extremely well.

There were seven hundred and eighty-three men in the battle line when it was formed on the high ground within a few hundred feet of the banks of the bayou. These forces facing each other across the distance of no more than a mile, were alien races that had clashed before in the centuries gone by.

As they fronted each other this day, they were in the struggle for the boundary line of distinct civilizations. Upon the discovery of the Americas, the Spaniard, by his explorations and bloody conquest, had fastened his dominion, his language and his laws on all South America, and at one time his claims covered more than half of North America. Even after the Spanish cession of Louisiana to France and the relinquishment of Florida to the United States, Spain yet held Mexico, and it included Texas and the vast country to the northwest to the 42nd parallel upon the Pacific. In North America, England had become the dominant power, and here on this April day there came the clash of Latin with Saxon sovereignty.

Sam Houston, Sidney Sherman, Tom Rusk, Edward Burleson, John Wharton and hundreds bearing English names and of English ancestry, were opposed to Antonio Lopez de Santa Anna, Castrillon, Juan Nepomuceno Almonte, Pedro Delegado and others bearing high sounding Spanish names. The ancestors of these combatants had fought each other when the Spanish armada sailed into the northern seas to work the destruction of England. And now they were come to grips in the contest for a land larger than the Continental Empire of Charles V, with the British Islands thrown in. One million square miles of river and forest, mountain and plain were lost to his Imperial Highness at sundown that day.

The destruction of the Mexican army was complete. Santa Anna, Almonte and Cos were captured, and Castrillon, who led the charge at the Alamo, was among the slain. Houston, on the 25th, made his official report advising that our losses were two killed and twenty-three wounded, six mortally.

Among the severely wounded was Alphonso Steele, who was shot through the lungs. Seventy-four years later, I met him on the battlefield—then the last survivor of the conflict. He related to me how he was shot down and thought his wound mortal, and that with a dying madness he took a fallen gun and killed a Mexican soldier who came within his range and then crawled to the rear to die, which he did seventy-five years after.

FAREWELL TO SANTA ANNA

Santa Anna was a coward, and however much one searches his long career of more than seventy years of active life for evidences of personal bravery or integrity, little trace of either will be found. One of his staff officers who afterwards wrote an account of the battle describes the Texas charge, and says:

> Then I saw His Excellency running about in the utmost excitement, wringing his hands, unable to give an order. Unable to give an order, nevertheless he did not wait for one to retreat, but left the field mounted on a splendid black stallion which had been taken from the Vince Ranch a few days before. In an effort to cross Vince Bayou, the horse was mired so that the President had to abandon him and continue his journey on foot. Houston had sent Deaf Smith just before the battle began to destroy the Bridge over Vince Bayou, across which the fleeing Mexicans now tried to escape; but for this Santa Anna on a fresh horse would have escaped and joined Filisola's command on the Brazos. In a report which was made to his government some years later, he says, "I alighted from my horse and concealed myself in a thicket of dwarf pines. Night came on and I crossed the creek with water up to my waist. I found a house which had been abandoned and some articles of clothing which enabled me to change my apparel. At 11 o'clock a.m. (the next day) I was crossing a large plain and my pursuers overtook me."

The next morning various parties were scouring the prairie picking up Mexican prisoners and all on the lookout for Santa Anna and Cos.

James A. Sylvester, who had come with volunteers from Ohio and who had worked as a printer on a Cincinnati paper, relates that, "We were near the bridge on Vince Bayou, and I saw some deer and rode nearer to get a shot at them, when they started. I looked to see what had frightened them and saw a Mexican going toward the bayou."

Not suspecting who he was, they took him into the camp, but his fellow countrymen recognized him in his disguise and from their exclamations when they saw him, his identity became known.

He readily agreed to issue an order to General Filisola, next in command, to retire to Victoria. "I have agreed with General Houston for an armistice until matters can be so regulated that the war shall cease forever."

The government ad interim, which retreated as far as Galveston Island, now reported for duty, and on May 14th concluded two treaties with Santa Anna, one of which was published, the other being a secret treaty. The open treaty provided that all hostilities should cease and that Santa Anna would not "exercise his influence to cause arms to be taken up against the people of Texas during the present war for independence."

In the secret treaty, he bound himself to "so prepare things in the cabinet of Mexico that the mission sent thither by the government of Texas may well be received, and that by means of negotiations all differences may be settled and independence acknowledged." The Rio Grande was to be the boundary, and Santa Anna was to be sent home at once via Vera Cruz.

These treaties were executed at Velasco and within less than three weeks after they were made, plans had been completed for sending the captive president home, and on June 3, 1836, he and his suite had embarked on the schooner *Invincible* at the mouth of the Brazos and were ready to sail, and he had issued a friendly farewell to Texas and the Texans.

Just before the vessel sailed, a steamer arrived from New Orleans bearing two hundred and fifty volunteer soldiers, who had come to take part in the Revolution. They at once determined that Santa Anna should not be liberated, and forcibly took him in charge, defying the government and setting aside as it were the treaties of Velasco. He was taken up to the Phelps plantation at Orozimbo, where he was held until the following November.

This ruffianism of our new friends is a chapter in our history which, like the land frauds of 1835, we would like to forget.

When the first Congress met in October, what to do with Santa Anna was one of the live questions, and one can well imagine how a legislative assembly would approach such a topic. He was prosecuted in the Senate and the House, and the speeches of Mosely Baker, Stephen H. Everett, the senator from Jasper, Vice-President Lamar and others, who would have hanged him, are powerful arraignments of his high crimes and misdemeanors. While the debate still ran high, President Houston assumed authority to cut it short by sending the captive home via Washington. On November 20, 1836, he and Almonte left the Brazos for New Orleans escorted by Bernard E. Bee, George W. Hockley and Wm. H. Patton. At New Orleans, Bee arranged for Santa Anna to cash a draft on Mexico for $1,000 to pay his expenses, and he permitted this draft to be protested, nor was it paid after his return home.

He went to Washington and conferred with President Jackson. While he was in the capital, the Mexican minister formally advised the Washington government that Santa Anna was no longer president of Mexico, and that his country would not be bound by any act or agreement of his.

After a very short stay in Washington, he sailed for Vera Cruz, and once at home he promptly resumed his career of intrigue, and with varied fortunes he figured in Mexican matters for many a year.

THE PASSING OF AUSTIN

The construction of a new government involved a vast amount of labor and detail, and a very large part of this work fell to the Secretary of State, and he entered upon his labors with his usual industry.

It was now fifteen years since he first rode down into the Colorado-Brazos country to select a site for his first colony, and since he lead the advance of his Old Three Hundred into the wilderness. He was only twenty-eight then. He had given these fifteen years to the enterprise, to the neglect of all else. For years he was the law of the colonies, and his firm, modest manhood had won for him and his people the respect of Mexico. He hoped to live in peace under the Mexican government, and was one of the few men in Texas who cherished the hope that Texas could and would remain a part of the Mexican Republic. A free people have ever been prone to cruelty and ingratitude towards those who have served them best. Athens banished Aristides the Just, as one of the Athenians put it, because he was tired of hearing him called the Just.

The Romans drove Cicero into exile, though the very best that now remains of the Roman literature and thought comes to us from the tongue and pen of Cicero. The history of our own country teems with conspicuous examples of men who have given their lives to the public service, and have been scourged into poverty and neglect in their old age.

Austin had been abused for ten years because he would not lend himself to mad schemes for a separation of Texas from Mexico. He was a reticent, silent man, and often misunderstood. William H. Wharton was his bitter enemy, and had often said ugly things about him. They were reconciled at the outbreak of the Revolution, and went together as commissioners to the States and became fast friends.

Upon their return in June, 1836, Wharton solicited him to become a candidate for the presidency. He was a man of prodigious energy. Almost at once after his return in June he took active steps to protect East Texas against Indian depredations, and was the instrument of procuring soldiers from the American army to be stationed at Nacogdoches.

He was not disgruntled by the fact that he only received a few hundred votes for the presidency, and gladly accepted a place with the administration, willing to help work out the national destiny of Texas, for Texas was his life labor and love. He had no family, and like Washington, Providence left him childless that his people might call him "Father."

During his long imprisonment in Mexico in 1834, and 1835, Santa Anna was in power, and on one occasion during this time had Austin brought out of prison for a conference regarding Texas affairs, and when the conference was over the jailer escorted him back to the bastille. And now a short year later when Austin returned from the States, Santa Anna was a prisoner at the Phelps plantation down in Brazoria, and Austin went to Orozimbo to confer with him about Texas affairs. When the conference was over, Austin rode back to his home at Peach Point and left his Imperial Highness in captivity.

As Secretary of State, his work required a vast amount of correspondence, which he conducted without the aid of an assistant. There were no typewriters or stenographers in those days, and when papers were written in duplicate as state papers must be, they were most laboriously copied just as they were first written.

The old State House at Columbia was little better than a barn, and here in a bare room, by the dim light of a flickering candle, he worked and wrote far into each night, preparing papers with instructions to our ministers and envoys, who were being sent on various missions far and wide. He sat on a chair with a rawhide bottom, and when the chill of the December night crept into the fireless room he gathered his cloak about his frail form and worked on, for there was much to do, and no other man living knew as much of Texas needs and affairs as the Secretary of State.

Just before the close of the year he sickened, and on December 27th he died of pneumonia. In the hours of his dying delirium, he lived over again the years that had gone before and his last words were, "Texas has been admitted."

And this brings us to the close of his eventful life, and the all-eventful year in Texas history. The Alamo had fallen March 6th; Fannin fell at Goliad on March 27th; San Jacinto was won on April 21st. Houston was elected President on September 3rd. The first Congress met on October 3rd. And in the last days of the year the great white soul of Austin went back to God who gave it.

THE REPUBLIC

THE REPUBLIC OF TEXAS

How strange and romantic the name sounds to this generation. Legally it began with the Declaration of Independence on March 2, 1836, but its existence was not assured until the Battle of San Jacinto in April. The span of its life ended on February 19, 1846, when it became a state in the American union after a national life of ten stormy years.

When Santa Anna was brought in a prisoner the morning after the battle, he issued an order to his scattered generals to fall back, pending negotiations for peace. The Provisional Government chosen by the Washington convention in March continued to function pending an election which was ordered held in September. Burnet, the president ad interim, and his advisors, concluded the treaties of Velasco with the captive Santa Anna on May 14, 1836, by which he agreed to use his endeavors to secure the recognition of Texas Independence with the Rio Grande as a boundary. This treaty was assented to by General Filisola, commanding the forces, and the invasion which had come with such pomp and circumstance in March sadly subsided in May, leaving His Imperial Highness a hostage for the good behavior of this country. The constitution which had been adopted in March was resurrected and submitted to the people for ratification at the September election, at which time the question of annexation with the United States was also submitted and a president, vice-president and congress chosen.

The constitution was ratified; Houston was chosen president almost by acclamation over Austin and Henry Smith, who received only a few hundred votes each. Lamar was elected vice-president, and only eighty-nine votes were cast against annexation. When we recall how diligently the Adams and Jackson administrations had wrought for years to accomplish the purchase of Texas, we would suppose that the Washington government would have immediately accepted this offer, and that annexation would have been accomplished in a few months at the furtherest. But for the first and last time in his long life, Jackson became a conservative, and the independence of Texas was not even recognized until nearly a year after San Jacinto (March 1837). The question of annexation is a chapter within itself, and when once fairly involved in American politics was delayed a decade.

Meanwhile the Republic of Texas moved on to its destiny. Houston was a great executive. He chose both Austin and Henry Smith for his cabinet and the new administration assumed control in October. The first congress of the Republic met at Columbia on the Brazos in a barn like building, which was destroyed in the 1900 storm, and which this generation remembers "like a ragged beggar sunning." In poverty almost pitiful the new government began upon the very tract of land where within the last few years the great Columbia oil fields were found, and more wealth has been taken from one of these wells than would have been required to pay the entire debt of the Republic during its whole existence.

William H. Wharton, who was a senator from Brazoria in the new congress, was named Minister to the United States, and Austin the new Secretary of State, entered actively upon the details of forming a government.

The first congress remained in session at Columbia until December, when it recessed to meet at Houston in the following May, this place having been chosen as the capital, until 1840. The people of Texas were very much disappointed that the congress of the United States did not at once reorganize Texas as an independent government.

When Minister Wharton reached Washington, he found many discouragements, but he at once set to work to urge his life-long Tennessee friend, Andrew Jackson, to agree to immediate recognition.

The end of the year was approaching, and as the holiday season drew nigh he haunted the White House, and at midnight on a bleak December night he wrung from the old warrior president a promise of immediate recognition; and on December 21st, while Santa Anna was in Washington, Jackson sent a message to congress recommending recognition, but the matter was delayed until the following March.

There were three constitutional presidents of the Republic—Houston, who served two terms, separated by the administration of Lamar, the second president, and Dr. Anson Jones, who was the chief executive when Texas was annexed.

The whole period of national life was filled with wars and rumors of wars. There was almost constant strife with Mexico, frequent spasmodic invasions. Twice large armies crossed the Rio Grande, and came as far as San Antonio, but nothing could tempt an invasion further east. In each instance they hurried back across the border before the Texans could rally to meet them.

But greater and nearer home than the Mexican menace was the ever-growing Indian hostility, provoked by the encroachment of the settlers upon the hunting grounds of the Red Brother north of the old San Antonio-Nacogdoches Road. The history of all that vast area is one of bloodshed, and every square mile of the land has its legend of Indian raid and massacre.

The Republic had a foreign policy, and sent ministers to foreign courts. It had an army and the usual strife and disorder of citizen soldiery. It had a navy which has a history of its own.

When the American congress offered Texas annexation, the question was submitted to our people in 1845, and was widely discussed throughout the state. There was a campaign, and mass meetings were held and public speeches made. A typical resolution was adopted at a mass meeting held in Richmond in June of that year.

RESOLVED, that like the prodigal son who had sojourned so long in foreign lands, we will return to our father's house.

On February 16, 1846, only a few days less than ten years from the birth of the Republic, Anson Jones, the last president, formally surrendered his authority, and J. Pinckney Henderson, the first governor of the State of Texas, began his administration.

The close of this era is well expressed in the words of President Jones, as he surrendered his executive authority to the governor-elect:

The Lone Star, which ten years ago arose amidst clouds over fields of carnage, obscurely seen for a while, has culminated, and following an inscrutable destiny has passed on and become fixed forever in the glorious constellation— the American Union. The final act of the great drama is now performed. The Republic of Texas is no more.

THE ARMY OF THE REPUBLIC

The charge was openly made in the United States by those who were unfriendly to the Texas Revolution, that there were not fifty citizens of Texas at the Battle of San Jacinto; that Houston's entire army was composed of volunteers and adventurers from the United States. William E. Channing, the Boston clergyman who lead a fervent crusade against Texas and the Texans, made this statement in his celebrated letter to Henry Clay, which was widely circulated as a political document during the annexation controversy.

It is true that the Revolution was wonderfully aided in every way by the people of the Southern states, and within three or four months after San Jacinto as many as twenty five hundred men from the States presented themselves for service during the war. It has been said on high authority that there were more men on the way to join Houston's command at the time the battle was fought, than he had with him. Touching the matter of foreign aid, Mr. Eugene C. Barker, who covered the topic in an article written for the Texas Historical Quarterly in 1906, wrote: "But when all is said it was really the old settlers who did almost unaided all the effectual fighting in the Texas Revolution. They captured Goliad in the fall of 1835, and assisted by a few companies from the United States, captured Bexar in December of that year, and practically alone they won the battle of San Jacinto."

It was also charged in those days that the Revolution was the work of what northern writers called the slave-holding oligarchy.

On November 11, 1836, there was pending before the first senate of the Republic a bill giving bounty lands to soldiers, and William H. Wharton, senator from Brazoria, made the point that the large land owners, the wealthy planters and merchants, were not at the Battle of San

Jacinto. "I have examined the list of those who won the battle (he said), and find that very few men who are esteemed men of property were there...I find that the battle was fought and won by the poor men of the country at least half of whom had never located a headright in Texas."

It has been said that nearly all of those who came to do military service remained in the country and became citizens. The news of the victory at San Jacinto caused a rush of volunteers from the States.

Felix Huston, a lawyer and planter, from Vicksburg, Mississippi, equipped five hundred men and brought them ready for service.

Memucan Hunt, from Mississippi, undertook to bring four thousand men, and was instrumental in procuring one thousand.

Thomas J. Chambers, of Texas, raised several companies in Kentucky, who came ready for service.

Rusk was named to command when General Houston left for New Orleans in May to get medical treatment for the wound he received in the battle. Rusk lead the army in the wake of the retreating Mexicans, and during the summer and autumn of 1836, it was camped at and near Victoria, and for several months afterwards on the Lavaca River.

After the Mexican forces were withdrawn, Rusk desired to be relieved, and suggested Felix Huston to succeed him. President Burnet named Colonel Lamar, who repaired to the army to take command. Felix was a convivial person, and had made himself so popular with the men in the service that they declined to accept Colonel Lamar, and he returned, leaving Huston in command.

A great many turbulent, meddlesome men foregathered with the so-called army, and little semblance of military discipline was maintained.

At one time a conspiracy was formed to depose President Burnet and try him at court martial for some feigned grievance, and a company of soldiers came all the way to the Brazos upon this fool's errand, but thought better of it.

All the while rumors persisted that another invasion was coming from Mexico, and though the army was a great financial burden as well as a menace, it could not be disbanded.

When the first congress met in the autumn of 1836, the army was its greatest problem. It was thought wise to name a man from the United States of military experience to command, and the two houses passed a joint resolution inviting General James Hamilton, of South Carolina, to become a citizen of Texas and commander of the army.

He had been an officer in the war of 1812, and had served as governor of South Carolina and United States senator from that state. General Hamilton declined the honor, and Felix Huston remained in command. "The Texan Army" of 1836 was a cosmopolitan affair, made up of men from everywhere.

Preston Johnston, in his life of Albert Sidney Johnston, describes them, "the ardent youth of the South, burning for military glory. Enthusiasts of constitutional freedom mingled with adventurers from Europe; souls as knightly and unstained as Bayard with outlaws and men of broken, desperate fortunes."

It was on the Coleto, in the summer of 1836, that the gallant Albert Sidney Johnston, lately a lieutenant in the army of the United States, and destined in the years to come to be one of America's greatest generals, joined the Texas army as a private. He was in his thirty-fourth year, and a splendid specimen of manhood. He remained with the army for a period, and served the new government in several minor capacities, and late in January, 1837, President Houston named him commander-in-chief of the army of the Republic, and he left Houston for headquarters on the Lavaca to take command. Felix Huston, though without military experience, had many qualities for a great commander, and among them was the esteem of his men.

When it was announced that Albert Sidney Johnston was coming to take command, both Felix and his friends felt that he had been badly treated, and were in an ugly mood. To make bad matters worse, Colonel Moorehouse rode over to Texana and met General Johnston as he came down, and was not over-careful in what he related about Huston's attitude and purposes.

On February 4th, Huston addressed a formal challenge to Johnston, professing respect and admiration for him, but remonstrating: "Your appointment was connected with a tissue of treachery intended to degrade me and blast my prospects...I therefore propose a meeting between us. My friend Major Ross will make all necessary arrangements."

No dueling pistols could be found in the camp, and they agreed to use Felix Huston's horse-pistols, and he gave Johnston his choice. The seconds arranged that they should fire from the hip, though General Johnston declared he did not think he could hit the side of a house with a hip shot. In the early morning of February 5th the little party forded the Lavaca and rode to an open prairie, where the principals stripped to their shirt sleeves and faced each other at sunrise,

There are two accounts of just what happened. Preston Johnston, in the biography of his gallant father, relates it: It is known to those familiar with the use of a hair trigger that if the finger is allowed to touch it, the report of another pistol will always produce a sufficient involuntary muscular contraction of the finger to cause a premature discharge. Availing himself of this fact, General Johnston raised his pistol quickly and with an eye on his opponent's trigger finger anticipated him enough to draw his fire before Huston could cover him with his pistol. Johnston repeated this five times with the same result. The sixth shot struck General Johnston in the hip.

Sidney Huston, a great grandson of Felix Huston, gave me a statement from an eye-witness who relates it thus: Johnston fired four shots, Huston three. The third time Huston's pistol snapped and he sat down, took his pocket knife and picked the flint of his lock and they took position for the fourth time, and when they fired Johnston fell.

Huston approached General Johnston as he lay wounded and offered his sympathy, and avowed his intention to serve under him, and indeed he remained with the army for some weeks, and cheerfully recognized Johnston as his superior officer. It was thought that Johnston's wound was fatal, and he lay near death for some weeks at the little village of Texana, but he lived for a wonderful military career, and died on the field of Shiloh nearly thirty years after. He and Felix Huston became fast friends, and Felix named a son for the great commander, and Preston Johnston wrote in his father's biography forty years later that "Felix Huston's character was brave and manly."

The problem of maintaining the army became more serious than the ever-threatening Mexican invasion, and, on April 18th, President Houston furloughed the first army of the Republic, and it passed into history.

THE FIRST CAPITALS OF TEXAS

The first grant made by the Mexican nation in April, 1823, directed Austin to select a central location for a city to become his seat of government, and Governor Garcia took the liberty of suggesting a name for the proposed city, and christened it San Felipe de Austin, San Felipe being his patron saint. It was named before it was located. The first site discussed was on the Colorado, near where Columbus was later located, but Austin chose the Brazos as more central to his settlements.

From 1823 to 1836 it remained the seat of government, and was the most important town in the colonies. When Houston's army retreated from San Felipe in April, 1836, going up the river to Groce's, the town was burned to keep anything of value from falling into the hands of the Mexicans.

Santa Anna reached there while the fires were yet smoldering, and reported finding it in ruins. The government was more or less migratory during 1836.

The convention which declared independence and set up the provisional government met in March at Washington on the Brazos, but left there, going to Harrisburg and then to Galveston. Burnet's headquarters were for awhile at Velasco and then at Columbia, where the first congress met in October, 1836.

It was determined to select a temporary capital, with the thought that the permanent seat of government should be located later and further north than the then existing settlements.

The two houses met in joint session on November 30th, 1836, to select a seat of government until the year 1840. The journal of this session recites that the following places were put in nomination: Houston on Buffalo Bayou, Matagorda, Washington, Velasco, Quintana, Nacogdoches, Hidalgo, Refugio, Fort Bend, Goliad, Groce's Retreat, Bexar, Columbia, San Patricio, Brazoria, Orozimbo. Upon the first ballot no place had a majority. Houston lead with eleven votes, Matagorda second with eight, and Washington seven. On the fourth ballot, Houston was chosen. On December 21st, the first session of the first congress adjourned to meet in Houston on the following May.

"Houston on Bufialo Bayou," as it is written in the congressional record, was yet a city in prospect when it was selected on November 30th for the temporary capital of the Republic.

The Allens, who promoted it, had surveyed the site in August, 1836, and on August 30th had inserted an advertisement in the Bordens' paper which spoke in florid terms of the site chosen upon which they proposed to build a city. They described its location, "The town of Houston is fifteen miles from the Brazos River, thirty miles from San Felipe, forty miles from Lake Creek, thirty miles southwest from New Kentucky, and fifteen miles by water above Harrisburg. Preparations are being made to erect a saw mill and a large public house."

As soon as it was chosen as the seat of government, interest in it was manifest. Ex-Governor Lubbock, in his memoirs published in 1900, tells of his advent here about January 1, 1837. He came on the steamboat *Laura*, which he declares was the first boat that ever reached her landing.

> Just before reaching our destination a party of us left the steamboat and took a yawl and went ahead to hunt the city. We found no evidence of a landing, and passed the site and ran up into White Oak Bayou, and got stuck in the brush. We then backed down the Bayou, and found that we had gone past the city, and a close observation disclosed a road or street laid off to the water 's edge.

> Upon landing we found stakes and footprints. A few tents were located not far away, one large one was used for a saloon. Logs were being hauled from the forest for the erection of a hotel where the Hutchins house now stands. (Now site of Southern Pacific building.)

The Allens had undertaken to provide a capitol building, and on April 16, 1837, they began its construction so as to have it ready for the session of congress, which was to and did convene on May 5th following. This structure stood at the intersection of Main and Texas, where the Rice Hotel now stands. And here at the appointed time, 12 o'clock noon, May 5th, 1837, the second session of the first congress of the Republic met. The indomitable Bordens with their newspaper followed the government from

Columbia, but were a wee bit late, and in the first issue of their paper, published in Houston on the 2nd day of May, 1837, they apologized for the delay.

> We left Columbia on the steamboat *Yellowstone* on April 16, but were delayed a week by the surf on the bar at Velasco. We were then stranded at Clopper's bar for a day, and reached Lynchburg on the 26th, whence we proceeded at the rate of one mile an hour to the head of navigation at Houston on Buffalo Bayou.

When Congress convened in Houston on May 5th, Robert J. Walker, United States Senator from Mississippi, was a guest of the houses. During the next decade, he was the stalwart friend of Texas, and one of the most powerful factors in bringing about annexation.

Austin Located at Waterloo

While the resolution which fixed the seat of government at Houston provided that it should remain the capital until 1840, yet the location of the permanent capital was an ever present interesting question.

By common consent it was agreed that the name of the city should be Austin, and almost the same consensus of opinion decided in advance that it should be located as far north as the old King's Highway, and on either the Brazos or the Colorado.

Though at the time there were few settlements in the dark and bloody ground north of the San Antonio Road, yet the frontier folks were pushing their perilous way into these wilds, and it was thought that the location of the seat of government there would make it a new center of settlement. The Second Congress, which met at Houston in September, 1837, named a commission to "inquire into the propriety of selecting a site on which to locate permanently the seat of government of the Republic."

This committee was instructed to select such a site between the Trinity and Guadalupe not further south than

Fort Bend or more than twenty miles north of the San Antonio Road. It made a report in November naming a number of places which it had considered, but without selecting one. No action was ever taken on this report, and in December, 1837, a second commission of five was named with instructions to examine various sites proposed and make a report in the following April, 1838. This committee reported that it had selected John Eblin's League, on the Colorado, adjoining the tract on which the town of La Grange was located.

The Second Congress, which was in session when this report was made, adopted it on April 17, 1838, and thus Eblin's League was chosen and Austin was to be located next door to La Grange in Fayette County.

Though President Houston had approved the resolution naming this commission in November, 1837, yet he vetoed the act of congress naming Eblin's League as the site in April, 1838, giving the reason that since the capital was to remain at Houston until 1840, it was premature to select a new site in 1838, for any intervening congress might at its will change it. It was generally thought that President Houston hoped the capital would remain at Houston.

There was a change in Presidents in 1838, and Mirabeau B. Lamar and David G. Burnet became president and vice-president.

The capital issue had been prominent in the campaign, and in January, 1839, Lamar approved a bill naming the third and last capital commission. The members of the commission chosen by congress were A. C. Horton, I. W. Burton, William Menefee, Isaac Campbell and Louis P. Cooke.

The act creating it stipulated that the site should be between the Trinity and the Colorado and above the San Antonio Road. The committee first decided in favor of placing the city on the Colorado, and in April, 1839, reported "that we have selected the site of the town of Waterloo, on the east bank of the Colorado." In their unanimous report they write: "The imagination of even the romantic will not be disappointed on viewing the valley of the Colorado and the woodlands and prairies at a distance from it, and the citizen's bosom will swell with honest pride when standing at the portico of the capital of his country he looks abroad upon a region worthy of being the home of the brave and free."

The village of Waterloo was then the home of four frontier families, and was far into the Comanche country. In May, 1839, Edwin Waller, who had been chosen to survey and lay out the new city, was well under way with his work, and, guarded by rangers, the construction work began at once, and was so far advanced that the government, headed by the president and his cabinet, reached Austin October 17, 1839, and was received with much ceremony, which ended in a banquet which began at 3 p.m. and ended when the president arose at 8.

Lamar was the chief factor in the removal from Houston prior to 1840, and tradition ascribes to him the selection of the beautiful site at the village of Waterloo. In Vol. 22 of the quarterly published by the Texas Historical Association, A. W. Terrell, who was long identified with public life in Texas, contributes an article which dignifies this tradition and makes it a part of our written history. Here is Mr. Terrell's narrative:

Lamar, then Vice-President of the Republic, came with a party of hunters in the autumn of 1837 and camped at an old fort in Fort Prairie, six miles below where Austin now stands.

Jacob Harrell was then the only settler living at the present site of Austin and no white man lived on the waters of the Colorado above him. His cabin and stockade, made of split logs, were built at the mouth of Shoal Creek, near the river ford. The hunters were awakened early in the morning by Jake Harrell's little son, who told them the prairie was full of buffalo. Lamar and his companions were soon in the saddle, and after a successful hunt were assembled by a recall from the bugler on the very hill where the capitol now stands. General Lamar sat on his horse and looked from the hill on the valley covered with rye; the mountains up the river, and the wonderful view to the south; and said to his companions, "This should be the seat of future empire."

When Lamar approved the act appointing the commission which made the final location, he asked them to go to Jake Harrell's cabin and look carefully over the site, and they did.

It is an interesting coincidence that Austin, some years before, had chosen this site as a location for his permanent home, where he hoped to retire and live his latter days in peace, although this fact does not seem to have been known to the committee which chose it to forever bear his name. There is yet in existence a letter which Austin wrote from Coahuila to Sam'l M. Williams in May, 1832, giving Williams instructions for surveying for him what he characterizes as "the most attractive spot in all Texas." The location is to begin, "at the upper line of Tannehill League about five varas beyond the Big Springs at the foot of the mountain," afterwards and now known as Mount Bonnel.

The survey was to include the "falls of the River."

He accompanied the letter with a sketch made from memory long after having visited this wild scene. "Here (he wrote), I shall fix my residence on the Colorado at the foot of the mountain to live."

His dream of retirement to this "most beautiful spot," was never fulfilled but his spirit may have lead the locators in 1839 when they went out into the wilderness to found the City of Austin.

THE COMING OF THE CHEROKEES

The native tribes of Indians in the timbered regions of Texas, when the first explorers came, were well disposed towards the white man, and indeed it is from one of these tribes of friendly folks, Tejas, that the name Texas comes.

But at the time of the coming of the first colonists, these native tribes were neither numerous nor formidable. This does not describe the Prairie Indian, as the Comanche and other tribe were called, who abounded in the vast region north and northwest of the old King's Highway. The story of the Cherokee, and his advent into and exodus from North and East Texas, is one of the sad chapters in human history. The ancestral home of the Cherokee lay about the beautiful Blue Ridge Mountains, and included the vast area watered by the rivers which flow from these mountains through Virginia, Tennessee, the Carolinas, Georgia and Alabama. The white man was crowding him out of these regions early in the last century, and President Jefferson thought to utilize some of the wild western lands acquired in the Louisiana purchase upon which to locate these and other Indians east of the Mississippi, who were hindering the progress of civilization.

Ten thousand Cherokees had migrated into Arkansas territory as early as 1809, and while Texas was yet a Spanish province about 1820, Cherokee tribes had come down into East Texas and applied to the Spanish authorities for land grants. They had come to understand that a man must have a paper title to hold land. When Stephen F. Austin was in Mexico in 1822, seeking a confirmation of the grant the Spanish authorities made to his father in 1821, Richard Fields, the chief of the East Texas Cherokees, was there urging a grant to his people. The most that Fields could get from the Mexican government was permission to occupy the land as it were during good behavior. This did not satisfy Fields or his people, and in 1825, when the Edwards and their followers brought on the so-called Fredonian Rebellion at Nacogdoches, they found the Cherokee leaders in an ugly frame of mind against Mexico for not having made them the land grant they had expected, and Fields and John Dunn Hunter made an alliance with the Edwards by which they were to jointly overthrow Mexican authority in Texas, and the Indians were to have the country north of the King's Highway—the San Antonio-Nacogdoches Road.

But when Fields and Hunter went back to their people to have them carry out the bargain, the warriors rebelled and murdered them both. The chief cause of the insurrection was the proposed alliance with the white settlers, for they foresaw that there could be no such thing as white settlements in an Indian country, and they hoped to make East Texas a Cherokee country.

Then, too, it subsequently developed that Mexican agents at work among them had promised Bowles, who succeeded Fields as chief of the Cherokees, that if they would depose Hunter and Fields that the Mexican government would reward them substantially, and it was called to Bustamente's attention that they hoped for a land grant in return for their loyalty. The Mexican authorities, including Teran, determined to make grants to the individual families of Cherokees, and there were negotiations for several years, and finally Colonel Piedras, commanding the Mexican garrison at Nacogdoches, was commissioned "to put each family composing the tribe of Cherokees in possession of the lands which they are now possessing." There were no instructions to issue them titles, and in fact it is apparent that the Mexican government never intended to do this, but rather to allow than to remain tenants at will, as it were.

Colonel Piedras and his garrison were driven out of Nacogdoches by the colonists in 1832, before he had executed this commission, and though they continued to press their claims, they never got more than permission to remain where they were until the Supreme Government should decide their case. In this way they were postponed from year to year, and the Revolution in 1835 found them occupying the country where they had dwelt since they first came into Texas fifteen years before, but with no paper title, and this they knew from past experience gave them an insecure footing.

It is estimated that the Cherokee and other East Texas tribes associated with them had more than 1,500 warriors and five times that many people at the outbreak of the Revolution. Their attitude towards the colonists at this time was one of grave concern, and in November, 1835, when it was known that a Mexican army was being massed for the invasion of Texas the following year, the consultation which we the provisional government of Texas, made a declaration to the Cherokees, "that we will guarantee them the peaceable enjoyment of their rights to their land as we do our own."

This declaration was made at the instance of General Houston, and he, John Forbes and John Cameron were named as commissioners to "take such steps as would secure the effective cooperation of the Indians." Houston and Forbes made a treaty with the Cherokees February 23, 1836, by which they were ceded a large territory.

There is no doubt that this treaty and Houston's great influence with these Indians (for he was a Cherokee chief) kept them from rendering aid to Santa Anna during the campaign of 1836. And there is less doubt that had these fifteen hundred warriors swept down through the settlements at any time after the fall of the Alamo, and before San Jacinto, the colonies would have been wiped out. All Texas was on the move in those days of the Runaway Scrape, and thousands of families would have fallen easy prey to these savage warriors while seven thousand Mexican soldiers were scouring the country from Bastrop to the sea.

During the present year, 1921, the Cherokees have undertaken to file suit in the Supreme Court of the United States for the recovery of these lands ceded them in this treaty.

THE PASSING OF THE CHEROKEES

The Cherokee was perhaps the most enlightened of all the North American Indians. They had a highly developed tribal government, an alphabet, a kind of rude literature, and had stern notions of individual property rights. Many of them were slave owners, and those who came to Texas in the early twenties were as well qualified for citizenship as the average Mexican of that period, who was himself an Indian of far less force than the Cherokee.

The fifteen years of fruitless effort they made to get title to their lands had made them suspicious of Mexico and of promises made them by Mexican officials and agents, while their great reverence for Houston had lead them into a treaty in February, 1836, which was the salvation of the colonists.

After San Jacinto the Republic refused to ratify Houston's treaty, and during his administration the Cherokees were left in the same suspense that they had suffered during the preceding fifteen years.

Suspicious of everybody and of the white settlers in particular, they were easily aroused and influenced by Mexican agents who were now sent among them, and began a series of offenses which led to their expulsion from the country in 1839. When Filisola retreated after San Jacinto under the armistice which Santa Anna had made, he took time to start intrigues with the Indians, sending agents among them to incite them to antagonism to the colonists, and these intrigues were kept up almost constantly for the ten long bloody years that elapsed before annexation and the Mexican War. It was not alone the Cherokees but the Comanches and various other tribes who dwelt in the vast country north of the old Kings Highway who were wrought upon and lead to take up the torch and tomahawk against the Texans.

But retribution came to the Cherokees first, to the others afterwards.

The story of the Cherokee expulsion has been often told, and I am going to briefly relate it here, taking the facts stated from the account given by John H. Reagan, who was in the fight. Reagan, who was a youth of twenty-one at the time, went with Lacy, the Indian Agent who was sent by President Lamar to notify the Cherokees that because of their repeated crimes against the whites and their continued intrigues with Mexican emissaries they must leave Texas, and go back to the territory of the United States, from whence they had come twenty years before.

When we reached the residence of Chief Bowles, he invited us to a fine spring near his house, where we were seated, and Lamar's message was read to him. Bowles said he could not answer as to abandoning the country until he could consult with his people, and he was given ten days. We returned to his house at the expiration of this time, and he said his young men were for war, and thought they could whip the whites, but he knew that in the end the whites would win. He said that while it was true they never had a title from the Mexican Government, yet General Houston had confirmed their right to the country by treaty.

He told of a plan he had on foot to join his tribe with the main body of the Cherokees in the States and take them all to California, and asked for time to gather their crops. (This was June, 1839).

Lacy told Bowles he had no authority to give him any such time. Bowles then said it mattered little to him, that he was now eighty-three years old and would not live much longer, but he felt a great interest in the future of his wives and children. That his tribe had always been true to him, and though he differed from them as to the course he pursued, yet they wanted war rather than go, and war it must be.

The colonists had determined upon their immediate expulsion, and three regiments were approaching: one lead by Rusk, another Landrum's Red Landers, and the third Edward Burleson's Regulars. While Rusk was waiting for the two other regiments to come up, Bowles was seeking delay so that warriors from other tribes might reach him, and Rusk and Bowles agreed upon a neutral line that was not to be crossed by either party without giving notice to the other. About sunrise on the morning of July 15th, John Bowles, a son of the Chief, and Fox Fields, son of Richard Fields, former Chief, rode to our camp and notified Albert Sidney Johnston that they were ready to move north across the neutral strip, and General Johnston thanked them and told them that the Texans would cross the Neches after them.

There were battles on the next two days, in which the Indians fought with great valour. Chief Bowles remained on the field on horseback, wearing a handsome sword and sash which had been given him by President Houston. He was a magnificent picture of barbaric manhood, and was the last to leave the field when the Indians retreated. He was wounded and his horse disabled, and he dismounted, and as he walked away was shot in the back and fell. Then as he sat up with his face towards us, I started to him to secure his surrender.

At the same instant my Captain, Bob Smith, ran towards him with a drawn pistol and we reached Bowles at the same instant. Realizing what was imminent, I called "Captain, don't shoot him," but he fired, striking Bowles in the head, killing him instantly.

This graphic account was written by Judge Reagan many years later, and we all know it is accurate.

The Cherokees moved north, and were subsequently joined with scattered remnants of their once powerful tribe, and located in the "Cherokee Nation." Judge Reagan says that besides Cherokee warriors, there were Shawnees, Delawares, Kickapoos and Indians from various other small tribes then living in North and Northeast Texas engaged in this battle.

General Houston was very bitter in his opposition to this campaign, and it brought down his great wrath upon the Lamar administration; and ever afterwards he held an almost savage hatred for Albert Sidney Johnston, whom he regarded as a strong instrument in bringing it about.

THE PRAIRIE INDIANS

Distinguished from the Cherokees and East Texas Indians, the many wild tribes who dwelt and roved further to the west were often referred to as the Prairie Indians, and the Mexican authorities were always hopeful that there would be no alliance between them. There were a number of these tribes, but the most formidable of them was the Comanche. It may well be doubted if this world has ever produced a more hardy, vigorous, terrible specimen of physical manhood and daring courage than the Comanche Indian. The Texas Comanche roved up and down the vast west from the Kansas prairies to the Gulf of Mexico, often taking side trips or excursions down into Mexico, where he always left a bloody trail. They rarely came east of the Lower Brazos, but there is not a village or hamlet west of the Colorado from Port Lavaca to the Red River that is without a tradition of his midnight visit.

He would come south in the winter along with the buffalo, which he called his cattle, and would seek the higher, cooler climate of the plateaus in the summer.

There was not a year after the first colonists came in 1821 that he did not depredate in the settlements, and during the Republic, stirred by Mexican agents and by the ever more obvious encroachments of the white settlers, he was a terror by day and by night. It was a custom of the Comanches after a raid into Mexico to stop by way of San Antonio and trade, and often after excursions into Texas settlements they would boldly come into San Antonio and offer their captives for ransom. On such occasions they would ride up to the commandant and require him to keep their horses and chattels while they went up town for a frolic. They made a kind of groom out of the small command which was depended on for garrison by the helpless population.

Albert Sydney Johnston was in San Antonio on one occasion in 1839 when a band of warriors came to town, and relates an interesting incident. Essowakkeny, the Comanche chief, dismounted, and pointing to his horses said, "There is our caballado, take care of it."

"Yes," said General Johnston, looking steadily at him. "You ride good horses; I take care of mine, you take care of yours." And the Indian met the fearless gaze of a warrior as bold as himself, and with a grim smile detailed some of his own men to watch his caballado.

The story of the Council House fight in San Antonio in March, 1840, has been often told, and is indeed one of the most tragic in the annals of our Indian wars. I have read many reports of it, some given by eye-witnesses, and the following is taken largely from the narrative of General Johnston:

In February, 1840, the Comanches agreed to bring all their white prisoners whom they were holding for ransom into San Antonio and deliver them to their families, and make a treaty with the Republic. Three commissioners were named by the government to meet the Comanche chiefs.

On March 19th, thirty-two warriors with their women and children came in for the pow wow. Twelve chiefs met the three commissioners at the stone Council House, and the talk was opened by the surrender of Colonel Lockhart's daughter, who had been captured at Gonzales the year before. Colonel Fisher, one of the commissioners, asked them where the other prisoners were, and they replied that she was the only one they had. The Lockhart girl then related that there were others in their camps whom they were holding back for larger ransoms.

Colonel Fisher told them of their wickedness, and demanded that they bring in the other prisoners, and named thirteen persons whom they were known to have captured within recent months. Turning full upon them, he said: "Do you remember murdering two men, and carrying away this girl (Miss Lockhart) when you were returning from Houston last year under a flag of truce?"

There was a silence for a moment after this challenge, when one of the chiefs arose, and standing his full height said, with haughty insolence, "No, we do not recollect," and sat down. There was another pause, and he rose again and defiantly said to Colonel Fisher: "How do you like our answer?"

Colonel Fisher replied, "I do not like your answer. I told you not to come here without all your prisoners; your women and braves may depart in peace, but we will hold your chiefs as hostages until the other white captives are brought in."

At this moment Captain Howard marched in a company of fifty soldiers. Instantly the Indians strung their bows and gave the war whoop. One of them sprang upon Captain Howard, striking him down with a knife. In the interval of a few seconds all the chiefs were slain. There were twenty warriors without the building and when they heard the war whoop inside, they all at once attacked the people, but all of them were killed save one, who escaped in to a house. Wishing to spare him, they sent an Indian woman to tell him that they would allow him to leave the house unmolested if he would go peacefully. He defied them, and refused their permission, and stepped from the building with his bow strung and ready for combat.

Mrs. Samuel Maverick, in her diary published many years after, relates that she, with a crowd of bystanders, was watching some small Indian boys who had come in with the party do some clever target shooting at a tree on the river bank. When the war whoop sounded and before the onlookers realized what it meant, one of these boys turned like a flash and shot an arrow into the crowd, striking a bystander in the heart. Years of terrible bloody warfare with the Comanches and their allied tribes followed this fateful day.

A quarter of a century later they were still on the warpath on the northwestern frontier, and my father was in many a battle with them. The year I was born, 1873, a party of Comanches murdered a family within a few miles of our frontier home.

THE SANTA FE EXPEDITION

Lamar's administration, 1838-1841, represented in most respects the very opposite of that of General Houston, which preceded it, and the second administration of Houston, which immediately followed. Houston would conciliate the Indians—Lamar would exterminate them. Their financial and foreign policies differed. Lamar would have a bank with certain restrictions—Houston, as the disciple of Jackson, regarded a national bank as a vile institution. General Houston was not eligible under the constitution to succeed himself in 1838, but he was during the entire three-year term of Lamar, a candidate to succeed Lamar, and during this interval was elected to the congress of the Republic, where he devoted himself largely to consistent opposition to the Lamar administration.

The ill-fated Santa Fe expedition was generally regarded as the greatest failure of Lamar, whose entire term was replete with disasters, due, however, in most instances to causes beyond the aid of statesmanship.

After the Revolution in 1836, Texas had always claimed the Rio Grande as its boundary and had been ambitious enough to contend for all the territory along that river to its source in what is now the Colorado, thence to the territory of the United States, and back in some indefinable way to Red River.

Word came to Texas in 1839 that the people of Santa Fe, which was on the east of the Rio Grande, hence technically Texas territory, were hostile to the Mexican government, and had rebelled and murdered a governor sent out from the City of Mexico.

Word also came that the inhabitants of that remote place and the environs thereabout might be induced to acknowledge Texas sovereignty.

There was much discussion during '39 and '40 of a proposed expedition to Santa Fe, and an effort to divert the large trade which was carried on between that region and St. Louis to some gulf port.

A bill was urged in congress for an appropriation for such a project, but it was defeated largely by the influence of Representative Sam Houston. Lamar determined, however, to send it anyway, and, early in 1841, named Hugh McLeod military commander, authorizing him to raise volunteers for the expedition.

President Lamar, who was great on proclamations, and, like another president we have seen in our own day, a brilliant writer, issued a salutary declaration, offering the people of that remote place the blessings of Texas citizenship, and it was sent ahead by one Dryden, an American merchant who had lately lived at Santa Fe. A commission was created to set up a government there when the people voluntarily accepted our proffered blessings, although the military were warned not to force submission upon these people, but to merely conquer them and set up a new government if they were willing to be conquered and have a new government. The commission was directed to take possession of all public buildings and governmental agencies, provided it could be done peacefully. With these impossible instructions, the expedition moved out on June 21, 1841, and took its long weary way across roadless wilds for nearly one thousand miles. There were about two hundred and seventy volunteer soldiers, accompanied by fifty odd merchant traders and other persons. In one month they made two hundred miles, and in September, after hardships almost unbelievable, they were in what is now New Mexico.

They suffered from drouth and for food, and were harassed by Indians, and late in September a detachment was sent ahead the main body limping along in the rear.

Governor Armijo, fully apprised of their approach, was on the lookout for them, and with a show of military force and through the treachery of a young lieutenant, Lewis, who was one of the Texas party, both divisions of the bedraggled expedition were induced to lay down their arms, which they did as an evidence of the perfectly pacific purposes for which President Lamar had sent them.

They were no sooner disarmed than all of them were started on foot as prisoners for the City of Mexico, in charge of a base brute named Salazar. Some died by the wayside from starvation and sickness. Others were murdered by their guards, and those hardy enough to survive a twelve-hundred-mile march under such circumstances were thrown into dungeons in the City of Mexico when they reached there.

After a time they were all released. George W. Kendall, one of the proprietors and founders of the New Orleans *Picayune*, accompanied the expedition from Austin, and after a long imprisonment was released in the City of Mexico the next year. In 1844 he published Kendall's *Santa Fe Expedition*, which is, from a standpoint of human interest and literary merit, the greatest book that has ever been written about Texas and the Texans. It created a great sensation in its day, and was widely read in America and Europe.

One reading it now after eighty years is charmed with its literary style and splendid narrative. His description of the journey across Texas, the capture near Santa Fe, the story of the tyrant Armijo, the long, terrible march to Mexico, and above all his wonderful glimpses of the City of Mexico after he was liberated by Santa Anna, should be read by every Texan of every generation. Taken at random from the pages of this wonderful book, I relate his story of Lieutenant Hornsby's ride:

> We were being marched along at a rapid pace and nearing Albuquerque when a single horseman was seen speeding across the fields.
>
> Soon he was up with the rear of our party, when checking his horse into a prancing canter, he politely raised his hat and addressed the prisoners as gentlemen while riding along the line. His horse was a beautiful black charger, and he a handsome young Mexican, dressed in green velvet trousers with a neatly fitting jacket *somewhat faded and worn.*
>
> The horseman rode twice up and down the line of prisoners, nodding gracefully as he passed, and eying the crowd as though in search of someone. Bye and bye his eye fell on Lieutenant Hornsby, the best dressed man among us. His Texas Dragoon jacket was new and his blanket was showy red.
>
> The cavalier at once checked his horse on seeing Hornsby, and asked the Lieutenant if he were tired. The long march had fatigued us all, and when Hornsby answered in the affirmative, the horseman bade him mount behind and said he would carry him a pace and rest his weary limbs. Instantly Hornsby was seated behind his new friend. In a moment the rider wheeled his horse, plunged heavy spurs into his flanks, and dashed away at a speed that was

truly amazing, across the fields, jumping irrigating ditches. We were being marched on towards Albuquerque, but as best we could, watched the fleeing figures until all we could see was Hornsby's red blanket disappearing in the distance. Later in the same day after we had been marched out of Albuquerque, the horseman reappeared bringing Hornsby with him and dropping him along the line galloped away. The Lieutenant wore instead of his Texas Dragoon coat, a half worn jacket much too small, and his showy red blanket was gone.

He related this story: A hard ride of three or four miles brought them to a house of somewhat neater construction than other Mexican dwellings. It was a solitary house half a mile from the road. Here they dismounted, and the Mexican politely lead the way into a room in which the furniture and appointments were luxurious. Scriptural paintings adorned the walls, and the sideboard bore decanters and cut glass, and the Lieutenant was invited to help himself to a decanter of brandy. At this moment the wife of the cavalier, a mild eyed woman, entered, and graciously lead the way to the dining room, where they all three partook of a splendid breakfast. Both husband and wife were assiduous in their attentions, and pressed dish after dish upon Hornsby with a most zealous courtesy. After breakfast the good wife brought cigarettes, and while they smoked the host opened the business which had induced him to invite the Lieutenant to his dwelling.

He had taken a fancy to Hornsby's neat fitting Texas Dragoon coat, and would exchange his somewhat faded and worn jacket for it. The guest protested he did not want to exchange his coat, besides, the proffered jacket was much too small for him. But the Mexican insisted, though the wife protested, and Hornsby was compelled to doff his coat and was helped into the ill-fitting, shoddy jacket, which he wore when he was returned to us. The Mexican then brought a heavy, coarse blanket and exchanged it for Hornsby's bright red one. Indeed this last exchange was a good one, for the heavier blanket well served the Lieutenant on his 1,200 mile tramp to the City of Mexico.

This business done, the Mexican indicated that he was ready to return, and the Lieutenant, now somewhat at home, walked to the sideboard and poured himself a stiff glass of brandy, and bowing to the host, tossed it off.

As they left the house to mount and ride, the wife followed, and gave Hornsby a large quantity of dried beef, and when her husband's eyes were away, stealthily slipped a quarter of a dollar into his hand and murmured, "Adios, Senor." And away they rode across the fields, and the Lieutenant was restored to us wearing a worn jacket much too small and without his red blanket.

HOUSTON'S SECOND ADMINISTRATION

One studying the history of Texas from the beginning of our era in 1821 down to the beginning of the Revolution in 1835, is impressed with the fact that it is a biography of Stephen F. Austin.

The annals of the second epoch, 1835 to statehood in 1846, are equally impressed with the great genius of Houston.

He became President a second time in December, 1841, and Edward Burleson was Vice-President.

The year 1842 was the most critical in the life of the Republic.

The country's finances were impossible. It had no credit at home or abroad. The Indians, stirred by the vigorous extermination policy of Lamar, but not exterminated, carried the torch along the whole frontier. The sad failure of the Santa Fe Expedition had brought gloom into every community in Texas and tears for some citizen who had gone with McLeod and whose fate was unknown.

Santa Anna, who was in power again in Mexico, sought this as a propitious time to increase hostilities, and in March a Mexican army under Vasquez suddenly appeared before San Antonio, and after occupying the city a few days, hurriedly retreated across the Rio Grande before a force could be raised to meet them.

But it is significant that in a very short time thirty-five hundred Texans were mustered from west of the Brazos and on the way to Bexar. But they were only minutemen, unable to leave their families for a campaign, and without military equipment. About the same time Mexican forces from across the lower Rio Grande came as far as Goliad. The fact that a Mexican army had come within eighty miles of the capital, and the constant inroads of the Comanches about Austin caused President Houston to convene Congress in June, 1842, in the City of Houston.

In September of this year a second invasion, lead by Adrian Woll, captured San Antonio and carried away many citizens. District Court was in session and the Judge and lawyers were taken along.

Woll made a move as though he would go on to Austin, but encountered a small force of about two hundred and fifty men under Colonel Caldwell a few miles out of San Antonio. Volunteers from nearby counties were hastening to the relief of Bexar, and one company of fifty-odd men rode out of La Grange lead by Captain Dawson, and came upon the rear of Woll's army. Unable to effect a juncture with Caldwell's men, Dawson's entire company were killed or captured in a bloody encounter fought on Salado Creek. Again the Mexicans learning that the country was aroused and men marching against them, scampered across the Rio Grande before a sufficient force could be mustered to meet them.

There was a wild shriek over all Texas for retaliatory war and an invasion of Mexico, and a command of about twelve hundred men under General Alexander Somervell marched as far as the border, but it was without supplies, or equipment for an offensive campaign.

All during the year volunteers from the States came into Texas in great numbers, hoping to be enlisted in a Mexican campaign. But the government was without means to care for or equip them, and in many instances they were desperate fellows, and when unable to go to war in Mexico made much trouble in Texas.

After some marches and counter-marches up and down the Rio Grande, Somervell's army returned home, but a small detachment of daring fellows would invade Mexico, and three hundred of them elected Captain William S. Fisher as their leader, and crossed the river and laid siege to the town of Mier. After hard fighting and many losses, they were compelled to capitulate to vastly superior numbers, and were started on a long journey to the City of Mexico. After many days the prisoners by concerted action managed to escape, but they were in the heart of Mexico, and were unable to reach the border, and one hundred and sixty of the original three hundred and four who had first crossed over for a conquest of Mexico were recaptured and brought up to a place where, under orders from Santa Anna, each tenth man was shot.

One hundred and sixty beans were put in a jar, one tenth of them were black, the others white, and the Texans were made to draw and those who drew black beans were forthwith shot to death.

The Mexican authorities were very anxious for the honor of martyrdom to fall on Captain Ewing Cameron, and he was made to draw first, but got a white bean.

After this decimation the remaining prisoners were started again for Mexico, and as they neared the city orders came to shoot Captain Cameron at once, and they were promptly obeyed. The remnant reached the capital while the Santa Fe prisoners were yet in dungeons. The frequency of Mexican raids upon San Antonio and the constant fear that Austin might be included in the next excursion made it unsafe to keep the seat of government there for a time, and Houston held forth at Washington on the Brazos, where he convened the regular session of the Seventh Congress in November, 1842. This aroused much ire among the frontier folks on the Colorado, who successfully resisted the removal of the archives. The greatest effort of Houston's second administration was to bring about annexation with the United States, which he cleverly aided by open negotiations with England designated to arouse the people in the States with the danger of English sovereignty in Texas.

Justin H. Smith, recently professor of Modern History in Dartmouth College, has written an elaborate work upon the annexation of Texas, and speaking of Houston at this epoch says:

> Endowed with a remarkably fertile and crafty mind, trained successfully as an American politician, finished in the school of Indian cunning, a gambler of long experience, a genius in the art of political histrionics, a diplomat whose only idea of method was to triumph and not be found out, a statesman able and determined, Houston worked in a situation beautifully adapted to facilitate the concealment of his aims.

A report made by a British agent to his government about this time said of him: "He is pure handed and manly, actuated by a grand ambition to associate his name with a nation's rise."

About this critical time in our history, John Tyler, President of the United States, initiated a move to annex Texas, which after three years of varying fortune triumphed in the closing hours of his administration. But the salvation of Texas in these gloomy years was the constant stream of immigration which flowed across its borders without ceasing, so that the thirty thousand at the time of the Revolution were one hundred thousand at the time of annexation.

ANNEXATION OF TEXAS

THE PROCLAMATION OF LA SALLE

The evolutions in history; the various changes in sovereignty through which Texas passed from the primitive plain and wilderness to statehood, must be of interest to this generation. "Not to know what happened before you were born is to always be a child."

It was a strange theory which the European nations employed by which each claimed portions of the Americas based upon exploration and discovery.

It never seriously occurred to any of these so-called civilized nations that the Indian inhabitants who had peopled these continents for countless ages had any title to their native land, any rights which need be respected. Strange even to romance are the events by which the fair land, which now bears the name of Texas, has passed from flag to flag.

There was a three-hundred-year race among the nations of Europe for possessions in the New World, each country basing its claims upon explorations and discoveries made by persons flying its flag. Spanish adventurers first reached the mainland through the Gulf of Mexico, and Spain's title to the Floridas was recognized because of explorations of De Leon and De Soto, about fifty years after Columbus' first voyage. Then there was a lapse of more than one hundred years after De Soto, on his fruitless gold hunt, discovered the Mississippi River, until La Salle, the Frenchman, coming from Canada, sailed down it to the sea.

On April 9, 1682, this enterprising individual stood on the west bank of the great river near where New Orleans is now located, surrounded by a small company of daring Frenchmen, and by a process verbal named and claimed the country far and wide for his monarch. They unfurled the flag of France, reared a rude cross, buried a plate, and in a loud tone of voice proclaimed the sovereignty of France over the lands traversed by the river and its tributaries, and christened the country Louisiana, for the "Grand Monarque," Louis XIV. How far this verbal proclamation reached, and what were the boundaries of the new province, were matters much debated, though never settled in the centuries to come.

Some said they crossed the Rockies to the northwest coast. Others that they extended east including west Florida. Others that they embraced all Texas down to the Rio Grande.

This last claim was given much force by the fact that La Salle came again to the Gulf Coast in 1685 and founded a colony on Matagorda Bay, and lost his life here in Texas.

After his death and the failure of his colony, the Spaniards through Mexico made feeble, futile efforts at settlements here, claiming the country as part of Mexico, but they succeeded little better than the French had done.

Another hundred years rolled around and Louisiana and Texas were yet wild, vast and unknown. France had made settlements in Canada, and controlled the St. Lawrence and the Great Lakes. The English had colonized along the Atlantic seaboard, and the Spaniard yet held the Floridas, and all Mexico, or New Spain, as it was called. There were some French settlements on the Mississippi, and New Orleans had become a port of some importance.

Then came the French and Indian Wars in the middle of the eighteenth century, and France and England fought for long bloody years over the valley of the Ohio.

Seeing that England would win, France hurriedly handed Louisiana over to Spain in 1762 to keep it from falling into the hands of England, and, curiously enough, Napoleon hurriedly sold it to the United States forty years later to keep it out of England's hands. And the United

States annexed Texas in 1845 to keep it out of England's hands. After this cession to Spain in 1762 and while Spain held Louisiana, the title to Texas was conceded to be Spanish whether it be treated as part of Louisiana or part of Mexico. At the close of the American Revolution, Spanish sovereignty was acknowledged over Louisiana, the Floridas, Texas, Mexico, and all the lands around the Gulf of Mexico. It claimed all of North America west of the Mississippi, and there was no one then to seriously dispute this claim.

But while the Colonies (now become the States) did not then covet more land, they did set great store by the right to navigate the Mississippi River. They claimed the country west to the river and south to the 31st parallel, or about to a line from Natchez, Miss, east, following certain objects to the Atlantic. Since, however, the lower river and its entrance to the Gulf ran through Spanish territory, it was a matter of much moment to have for the people of Kentucky and Tennessee and all the territories west of the Alleghenies the right to navigate the river to its mouth and reach the Atlantic seaboard by way of the Gulf.

After some years of negotiation, a treaty was concluded in 1795 between the United States and Spain, giving us the right to navigate the river, and depot facilities for goods on the west bank of the river at New Orleans. For the time being this seemed all our country could want. The close of the eighteenth century saw England in control of Canada, and the United States of the country to the Spanish possessions south and west, and Spain the nominal master of the greater part of North America.

Thus far little detail had been given to boundaries, and fully four-fifths of all North America was uninhabited and more than half of it yet unexplored. Texas was little more than a name on a map at the close of the eighteenth century. In a feeble way Spain had exercised a nominal authority over the country for a century or more, and in an effort to reclaim it had built missions at various places where Franciscan Fathers labored to tame and save the Red Brother. But the Indian did not take kindly to being tamed and saved and the missions were failures. Some of them still stand after another hundred years have rolled around, the last mute evidence of Spanish sovereignty.

NAPOLEON'S FIRST EFFORT AT KING MAKING

The dawn of the nineteenth century saw strange things transpiring throughout the world, and perhaps the strangest was the case of the young islander who had come to France and during the Revolution made himself master of that bloody, turbulent country.

Napoleon, then thirty years old, was First Consul of the Republic, and planned to become, as he shortly afterwards did, and Emperor. He had lately led victorious armies in Egypt and Italy, and assumed a mastery over the Italian cities and states. Down in Italy not far beyond the Alps was the old Roman City of Parma, which had withstood the wars of centuries and had been made a dukedom or Duchy by some of the Popes four hundred years before. In the course of the eternal conflict which had prevailed among the so-called great powers of Europe, this had become an appendage of the Spanish Crown, and at this time the Duke of Parma was the nephew and son-in-law of Charles the IV, the Bourbon King of Spain.

The Duke of Parma wanted to be a king, and this fact was related to Napoleon, who had the same ambition on a larger scale. And it suited the purpose of this strange, restless person to make a king out of this degenerate Bourbon Duke. So that it came to pass that a kingdom, warranted to contain not less than one million souls, was created by Napoleon in Northern Italy about Parma, and named Etruria, following in part the boundaries of a Roman province of the same name. And the young Duke of

Parma and his pretty little Spanish bride, the daughter of twenty kings, came down to Paris to apply to Bonaparte, the Republican First Consul, for a kingdom and a crown. Amidst festivities and gaieties such as have often prevailed in Paris, Napoleon began his career as a king maker, and made this youthful pair King and Queen of Etruria, and bestowed upon them the hereditary title of Rulers of an Italian Kingdom of one million human souls over which he had no semblance of right to rule, and yet less to bestow upon others as a bounty. But the Duke of Parma was happy to be a king, and his pretty little Spanish bride, daughter of so many kings, was glad to be a queen, and the young Corsican was glad to begin the experiment of setting up kingdoms and making kings, for that was to be his chief occupation in the years to come.

But in the hurried recital of these interesting things, I almost overlooked relating an incident, for such it was. Napoleon exacted a fee from the Spanish King for the bounty of this Italian kingdom of one million souls, and King Charles, who was land poor, gave him Louisiana.

And so it happened on October 1, 1800, that the Secret Treaty of San Ildefonso was signed (for this was before the blessed day of open covenants), and his Catholic Majesty receded all of Louisiana to France, from whom Spain had acquired it forty years before. And the wild province which had been proclaimed and named by La Salle to embrace all the lands traversed and watered by the Mississippi and its tributaries became French again. What were the boundaries of the vast realm bartered for a petty Italian kingdom? Some said they crossed the Rockies to the northwest coast. Others that they extended east and embraced west Florida. Others that they embraced all Texas down to the Rio Grande. And so it happened that Texas and some ten other of our now American states were lightly bartered to make a petty duke a petty king in a land thousands of miles from these shores.

The Louisiana Purchase

Rufus King, our Minister to England, heard rumors of the secret recession of Louisiana to France in return for an Italian kingdom, as early as March, 1801, and wrote to James Madison, our Secretary of State, advising of the report.

Our ministers to England, France and Spain were at once charged to learn the facts, for this country was deeply interested in the affair. But the contracting parties were very reticent about giving out information, and though Chancellor Livingston, our Minister to France, was very diligent and inquisitive, it was nearly a year before he had a first hand confirmation of the secret bargain.

President Jefferson was much moved by the danger of a powerful neighbor in control of the Lower Mississippi. In April, 1802, he wrote Livingston: "There is on this globe a single spot the possessor of which is our natural habitual enemy. It is New Orleans, through which the produce of three-eighths of our territory must pass to market. France placing herself in that door, assumes to us the attitude of defiance. Spain might have retained it quietly for years. Her feeble state is such that her possession of the place would hardly be felt by us and it would not be long before *some circumstance might arise* which would make the cession to us worth her while. The day France takes possession of Louisiana, we must marry ourselves to the British fleet."

Then came a long year of negotiations for the purchase of a site at the mouth of the river. Livingston was unable to get the French statesman to talk to him with any freedom. At one time after the terms of the treaty of San Ildefonso were generally known, Talleyrand sought to deny to Livingston that France had acquired Louisiana, and advised him to apply to Spain if he wanted to purchase any part of the territory. Just at this juncture the Spanish Intendant at New Orleans aggravated matters very much by annulling the treaty of 1795 between the United States and Spain, and closing New Orleans to ships bearing American merchandise and products.

This caused a tremendous stir in all the western country, and Livingston promptly advised Talleyrand that since Spain still owned Louisiana, as he intimated, we would know how to deal with her, and if she would permit a petty official at New Orleans to annul a national treaty, we would take possession of the port and open it to our commerce and deal with Spain on the ground. This prompt direct statement soon brought an admission that Louisiana had passed back to France, but they said that it was not for sale. The act of the Spanish Intendant at New Orleans in 1802 annulling the privilege of depot facilities for American goods, caused much excitement in the United States, and President Jefferson knew that if this country could not purchase New Orleans and the unrestricted right to use the Lower Mississippi, that it would only be a matter of a few years when the westerners would take it by force. In fact a resolution was offered in the United States Senate suggesting the latter course, and it was only kept from passage by assurances that the administration was using every effort to reach an agreement with France and Spain.

In order to give due emphasis to the activities that were being put forth to accomplish this result, Jefferson named James Monroe, of Virginia, Envoy Extraordinary to France and Spain, charging him to hasten negotiations for the purchase of New Orleans and the Spanish territory east of the Mississippi River.

In all the correspondence that passed between our government and Livingston and Monroe during these long negotiations, there was scant mention of the territory west of the Mississippi and north of New Orleans, for no one was interested in it. In one letter it was suggested that if we had to purchase it, we might be able to sell it for enough to recover the price paid for the whole. Napoleon was a visionary person at thirty, and had many schemes for the use of Louisiana.

At one time he was going to found a vast colonial empire, and an expedition was being fitted out for that end. Livingston wrote Madison in March, 1802, "It is a darling object of Napoleon, who sees in it a means to gratify his friends and dispose of his armies."

But just then his eternal quarrel with England renewed itself, and it was currently reported that the British government was planning an expedition to occupy New Orleans. This quickly determined him to employ his colonial expedition in his war with England and to hurriedly sell Louisiana to the United States, to keep it from falling into English hands.

Forty years before, when France and England were nearing the end of the French and Indian Wars, and it was evident that England would triumph, and after Canada had been taken from the French, Louisiana had been hurriedly ceded by France to Spain to keep it out of English hands, and now for the last time it was bartered about in the political game of European nations.

And the country that had been claimed and named by La Salle in his verbal proclamation made at the mouth of the Mississippi one hundred and twenty years before, and that had been bartered back to France for an Italian kingdom, became a part in the United States of America.

TEXAS TRADED FOR FLORIDA

During the centuries since the English, Spanish and French explorers had first come into North America and laid the claims of these nations to the continent, there had been no settlement of the western boundaries, and no one could say with any approximate accuracy what was included when France ceded Louisiana to Spain in 1763, or when Spain receded it to France in 1800, or when it was sold to the United States in 1803. Livingston asked the French diplomats if the Spanish cession to France at San lldefonso had included the Floridas, and they told him they supposed so. Pinckney, our Minister to Spain, made the same inquiry at Madrid, and was told they supposed not. No one seemed to know or care very much.

Livingston wrote in 1802, while negotiations for purchase were pending; *As part of the territory of Spain, Louisiana had no precise boundary, so it is easy to foresee the fate of Mexico.* The boundary between Canada and Louisiana is alike unsettled."

While there was much concern as to how far east Louisiana could be extended, no one connected with our government in these negotiations seemed to care a rap how far north and west it went. Livingston wrote President Jefferson in October, 1802: "Joseph Bonaparte asked me whether we would prefer the Floridas to Louisiana, and I told him we had no wish to extend our boundary across the Mississippi;" and again in 1803, he wrote: "Talleyrand asked me today if we wanted the whole of Louisiana, and I told him no, only New Orleans and the Floridas."

In fact Jefferson and Madison wanted nothing but the mouth of the Mississippi River and west Florida, through which the rivers from our then western and southern states flowed to the Gulf.

At one time it was suggested by Livingston that the Island and City of New Orleans be made an independent state under the joint sovereignty of France, Spain and the United States, in which event this country would not be further interested in the purchase of Louisiana.

When Monroe reached Paris in 1803, Napoleon had indicated to Livingston his willingness to sell, and insisted on selling the whole territory, so it happened that our Ministers had it fairly forced upon them.

After the bargain was closed, Livingston was much worried for fear the Washington government would censure him for having agreed to take the country west of the Mississippi River.

On May 13, 1803, a few days after the treaty was signed, Livingston and Monroe wrote Madison an apology for having accepted the whole territory. "We well know (they wrote) that the acquisition of so great an extent was not contemplated."

But they pointed out that they were unable to escape taking it all without endangering the whole negotiations, that Marbois, the French Minister, was obdurate. And when after concluding the bargain, they came to examine Monroe's commission, they found it restricted him to the purchase of territory east of the River, and this gave them a new fright. But Jefferson and Madison were indulgent and did not complain at them for having been bullied into accepting nearly one million square miles more than they were instructed to buy at the same price. Jefferson wrote a friend that he might use this western country for the Indians and move those east of the Mississippi upon it. But what were its boundaries? The American ministers were unable to get any definite statement from France about boundaries. They would be told that France got from Spain in 1800 the same territory that it ceded Spain in 1763. Livingston, in his diary of events surrounding the purchase, says:

"I asked the minister what were the east bounds of the territory ceded to us." "He said he did not know, we must take it as they had received it." "I asked him what Spain meant to put them in possession of and what they had meant to take from Spain." He said, "I do not know, construe it in your own way. You have made a noble bargain, make the most of it."

The American government felt that the purchase extended to the Rio Grande on the southwest, and included West Florida on the east, but was so much more interested in Florida than in Texas that little thought was given the latter. The Spanish government was much disappointed at learning of the sale of Louisiana to the United States, and the Marquis d'Yrujo, Spain's Minister to the United States, addressed a series of notes to Secretary Madison declaring that France had no right to sell the territory. Madison mildly but firmly told the Marquis to tell his troubles to Napoleon, and the incident was closed. Spain did not relish the United States as a next door neighbor, and set about to hold Texas as part of its Mexican possessions.

In order to keep Americans out, it was planned to have a vast area between the two countries filled with Indians, who would be friendly with Mexico but hostile to the American settler.

The Jefferson administration was contented with the acquisition of Louisiana. The days of Madison, who succeeded, were largely filled with other matters, including the war of 1812.

When Monroe became President, he bent his energies to the acquisition of the Floridas with the hope of getting Spain forever out of the territory east of the Mississippi. When the De Onis treaty was before the Senate, Henry Clay stated that by right the Louisiana purchase included Texas to the Rio Grande, but neither he nor anyone else seriously objected to giving up Texas for Florida.

The De Onis treaty of 1819 gave the United States Florida and released Spain's claims to all land north of the 42nd parallel, the northern boundary of California.

In return the United States gave up its claim that Texas was part of the Louisiana purchase, and for the time being all claim to the country west of the Sabine and South of Red River was relinquished. And so it came to pass that Texas, which was in fact a part of the Louisiana purchase on account of La Salle's explorations, was relinquished in 1819, to be reclaimed by American frontiersmen in 1821-1836 and re-annexed to the American Union in 1836-1846.

The story of that annexation is one of the most interesting in our political annals. By almost unanimous vote, the people of Texas offered to enter the American Union at the first election held in 1836. This offer was rejected by Congress in 1837, under the great pressure brought by the abolitionists. So overwhelming was this defeat that all hope of annexation seems to have died out for the next five years. In 1843, President Tyler started a crusade for that result, which he pushed with great vigor until the close of his term in 1845, when he succeeded in getting favorable legislation through Congress only a few days before he surrendered office to Polk. The annexation of Texas was the largest question before the American people from 1843 to 1846, and was the paramount issue in the presidential campaign of 1844.

It kept Henry Clay out of the presidency and was the rock which wrecked the Whig party. It defeated the nomination of Van Buren at Baltimore in 1844, and brought about that of James K. Polk, the first "dark horse" ever named for the presidency.

It resulted in the keenest diplomatic game ever played on this continent, in which the frontier folks won over the representatives of England and France. It stopped the aggressions of England in North America, and played a powerful part in the acquisition of Oregon, and last, but not least, it resulted in a war with Mexico which carried our flag to the Pacific. This generation can well review in some detail this great stirring chapter in the history of the world.

First Efforts at Re-annexation

Jefferson had purchased Louisiana, and Monroe had acquired the Floridas, and so when John Quincy Adams became president in 1824, he was anxious to do his bit in extending our boundaries. He was aided in this ambition by no less person than Henry Clay, who was his Secretary of State.

The first American Minister to Mexico after that country became free from Spain, went with instructions to open negotiations for the purchase of Texas down to the Rio Grande. Secretary Clay gave him a schedule of prices to offer for the country to the Rio Grande, or to the Nueces, or to the Colorado, or even the Brazos, and furnished him with arguments to advance why Mexico should sell.

One of these was that the Comanche Indians who infested the country could be sold with it, and the responsibility of diplomatic relations with these war-like folks would pass to the purchaser, that the United States would take the land with the encumbrance, so to speak.

Though these advancements met with no favor in Mexico, Clay and Adams continued them during their entire administration. When General Jackson became president, succeeding Adams, he was even more zealous for the repurchase of the land which Monroe had given up for Florida, and for eight long years, even up to San Jacinto, the American Minister in Mexico kept up the scheme of buying Texas. The President was ably aided by his skillful Secretary of State, Martin Van Buren.

During those years, 1825-1837, it seemed conceded in the States that the acquisition of Texas was devoutly desired by all. The Texas colonists fresh from the States came imbued with this idea, and when separation from Mexico was in prospect in 1835 and '36, the people of Texas naturally expected to be incorporated in the American Union without delay.

When the Colonial Convention met at Washington on the Brazos in March, 1836, and a government was organized and a constitution written, a resolution was passed providing for the submission to the people of the question of annexation to the United States, at the same time the constitution was submitted for ratification. This was done at the September election held in 1836, when Houston was elected president and the constitution ratified. Only eighty-nine votes were cast against annexation.

But the San Jacinto campaign and the capture of Santa Anna had turned the eyes of all the world on Texas. Mexico bitterly complained to Europe that the United States had backed and fomented the Revolution to get Texas. Companies of soldiers had been openly equipped and had marched with flag and drum out of many American cities to aid Texas in its war for freedom, and the Revolution was furnished and financed in the United States. These things were pointed to by suspicious persons in Europe as well as Mexico as an evidence that the Washington government was an instigator of the Revolution. This lead the government to issue a neutrality warning, the effect of which may be fairly seen in the case of Captain Grundy, United States District Attorney, who was raising a company in Nashville for service in Texas. He issued a terrible warning: "I have orders to arrest and prosecute every man who may take up arms in the cause of Texas or in any way violate United States neutrality," said he. "I will prosecute any man in my command who takes up arms in *Tennessee* against Mexico, and I will lead you to the border to see that our neutrality is not violated as long as we are *on our soil.*"

The people of Texas were therefore little prepared at the reception they got in the United States in 1836 and during the Van Buren administration which followed Jackson.

At first the atrocities of the Alamo and Goliad had aroused the American people to a frenzy, and the quick success at San Jacinto to an enthusiasm, both of high degree. Benton of Missouri declared in the United States Senate that Houston was the first general since Marc Antony who had captured the head of a government and chief of an army in a single stroke.

Henry Clay, late secretary to John Quincy Adams, and now a senator, made felicitous remarks, and offered a resolution in the United States Senate hinting at the recognition of Texas independence.

But the "tumult and the shouting" soon died, and at home and abroad forces antagonistic to Texas and the Texans were loosed, so that instead of immediate annexation, as all Texas hoped, even recognition was only gained after a long, bitter fight of a year, and annexation, deserted by its former friends and fought by the fanatic forces of abolition, was delayed for ten long years.

Even President Jackson, who during eight years had continued to dicker for the purchase of Texas, and who spent his closing years working for annexation, turned conservative when the Texas agents arrived in 1836 and began their overtures for recognition and hints at annexation. He reminded them that the United States had treaty obligations with Mexico which must be observed, and expressed regret that the people of Texas had voted for annexation before its independence had even been recognized. When strong, stern men like Jackson wavered, what could be expected of the average American politician of the Van Buren type?

It may be doubted whether the American Congress would have voted recognition when it did in February, 1837, had not the Mexican Minister to the United States acted the fool. He bullied and talked too much, and finally asked for his passports and went home. Jackson thought it was enough for him to bring about recognition, and suggested that annexation, which he devoutly wished, be left to a northern president.

He went out of the office in March, 1837, and retired to his home in Tennessee. But he devoted the closing years of his life to the consummation of annexation, and it may be truly said that Ex-President Jackson and President Tyler were the greatest individual forces in the United States in bringing this result.

TEXAS REJECTED IN 1837

Martin Van Buren, of New York, became President of the United States in March, 1837, and the Congress which assembled in that year wrestled mightily with the annexation of Texas. The American Anti-Slavery Society set itself to the task of preventing it at any cost. Petitions and memorials circulated and signed by abolitionists poured upon Congress in such numbers that a member said they could only be measured by the cubic foot. It was said that in this single session six hundred thousand signatures were presented against annexation. Channing, the Boston clergyman, circularized the country in wild outbursts against extending our sovereignty to the southwest.

John Quincy Adams, who as Secretary of State to Monroe, declared the greatest event of his life was the signature of the De Onis treaty, by which we acquired Florida, and who as president schemed for four years to acquire Texas, was now (in 1837) a member of the House of Representatives, and wrote in his diary: "The annexation of Texas to the Union is the first step to the conquest of all Mexico, of the West Indies, of a maritime, colonizing, Slave-tainted monarchy, and of extinguishment of freedom."

And the old man did not confine his activities to mere entries in his diary. When the resolution for annexation came before the House in that year, near the close of the session, the venerable ex-president made a three weeks' address in opposition to it, which closed the session and defeated the measures. A similar resolution introduced by Senator Preston of South Carolina, in the United States Senate, was defeated by a vote of twenty-four to fourteen.

This seemed the death knell of annexation, and its enemies accepted it as final. In Texas all hope was abandoned and our people prepared themselves for an independent career. The question seems to have died out so completely for the next five years that neither in Congress nor in the American papers was there any serious mention of it. In 1842 there was a spasmodic revival when it was known that Senator Walker, of Mississippi, was about to offer a bill for the project. But he got so little encouragement that he did not do so. The benevolent liberator, William Loyd Garrison, declared at this time: "It is impossible for any honest man to wish success to Texas. All who sympathize with that pseudo-Republic hate liberty, and would dethrone God."

During these years, 1836 to 1842, Texas went through a dark and gloomy period, weak at home and derided abroad. The sympathy stirred by the struggle of 1836 was forgotten. Mexican influence in Europe was exerted to the utmost against us. In the States we had left only a few friends in the South. The Van Buren administration inherited the financial follies of Jackson's regime, which follies did not reach high tide until the Panic of 1837.

Fortunes were swept away and the wild speculation of the day of inflated currency left many a Southern planter and slaveholder bankrupt. In those days of monetary disaster, Texas became an asylum for many a fugitive debtor.

I was trying a lawsuit at Richmond, Texas, twenty-odd years ago, and a very old negro was a witness. They were proving by him some dates long before the Civil War, and he gave the year and month that his old master had brought him to Texas, when he was a small boy. I asked Uncle Remus how he remembered these things of so long ago, and the grey, garrulous relic of another day assured me: "We left Virginia in the night, suh, Marse Thomas and all his niggers, and we traveled mostly in the night until we crossed the Mississippi River."

So general had this exodus of fugitive debtors became, that throughout the southern states sheriffs would return writs of attachment and execution, with the simple notation, "G. T. T.," which meant "Gone to Texas." Back in the States, Texas was regarded chiefly as a refuge for runaway debtors. During these troubled years Mexico, always torn by its own revolutions, was never able to fit out an expedition to re-conquer Texas but would continually send marauding forces across the river to plunder and harass our people, and twice these invasions came as far as San Antonio, which was captured and plundered. The Texans made several attempts to retaliate by invading northern Mexico, and when they did so the abolitionist press of the North would scream out: "That we were a nation of freebooters and pirates, molesting a peaceful neighbor nation."

Massachusetts was the ex-officio arch enemy of Texas and the Texans, and from it radiated such sentiment as found in Garrison's utterance above quoted, "that one who would befriend Texas, would dethrone God." John Quincy Adams, of Boston, spent his last days going up and down New England in a scream of wild frenzy. He spoke softly and kindly of Mexico, the Mother Country, robbed of its provinces by filibustering Texans, and closed his appeals with the declaration: "No act of Congress or treaty of annexation can impose the least obligation upon the several states of the union to submit to such an unwarrantable act, or to receive into their family such misbegotten and illegitimate progeny. The admission of Texas would be identical with the dissolution of the Union."

A Boston daily paper about the same time wrote: "We have territory enough, bad morals enough, public debt enough, slavery enough without adding Texas." Texas, under the pressure of such propaganda, sunk low in the world's esteem. Doctor Stephen H. Everett of Jasper County, one time a Senator of the Republic of Texas, made a trip through the States in 1842, and upon his return reported: "Texas in the Northern and Eastern states stands as low in the grade of nations as it is possible for a nation to stand and exist."

Van Buren was defeated for re-election in 1840 by the Whig candidate Harrison, but the Texas question was considered so dead after 1837 that it was not an issue in the 1840 campaign. Sam Houston entered upon his second term as President of Texas in 1842, and he found the fortunes of Texas at a low ebb. Despairing of help from the United States, he turned his attention to a European alliance, and with a skill rarely equaled in diplomatic history, he played a game with England which was the chief factor in reversing the policy of the States. Oddly enough France had thrown Louisiana, which included Texas, to Spain in 1762 to keep it out of England's hands, and Napoleon passed it to the United States in 1803 to keep it from England, and now forty years later, after many changes of sovereignty and fortune, the fear of English domination drove the United States to take Texas and wage a war with Mexico. Indeed it seems that old England has played a powerful part in our destiny.

PRESIDENT TYLER DISCOVERS TEXAS

In 1842, John Tyler of Virginia was President of the United States. A Democrat out of harmony with his party, he had been elected Vice-President by the Whigs, and when William Henry Harrison died after a few weeks' incumbency this Virginia Democratic Whig ruled in his stead. The Democrats despised him as an apostate, the Whigs as an interloper, but he was a man of long political experience and no little political acumen, and he set his heart on the annexation of Texas.

Nothing short of the power and prestige of the presidency would have sufficed to enable an advocate of Texas annexation to make any headway in the United States in 1842 to 1844, in the face of the terrible defeat in 1837, and the apparently overwhelming sentiment against it at this time. A president, backed by the party that elected him, would never have dared to hazard his party's success by espousing this dead, dangerous issue.

But Tyler had no political expediency to impede him. Hated alike by Democratic and Whig leaders, he knew his political fortunes lay along lines hostile to them both. It was generally conceded as early as 1842 that Henry Clay would be the Whig candidate for the presidency in 1844, and that Ex-President Van Buren would be the Democratic candidate. It was also known that the leaders of both parties devoutly hoped that the Texas question would remain dormant in 1844, just as it had in 1840 in the contest between Van Buren and Harrison. There were strong Southern leaders like Calhoun, Walker of Mississippi, and others, who were always open champions of annexation, but no one in power with either party, no party leader, was willing to stand out for it, nor were they anxious to have to stand out against it. They simply hoped it would not be injected into the coming campaign, which was already well on in 1842.

But John Tyler was a nervous, energetic, active person, and he loaned all his energies and staked his political fortunes on a campaign to "re-annex" Texas.

Every member of his cabinet except Daniel Webster, who was Secretary of State, resigned when he vetoed the Whig Bank Bill in 1841. But when Webster later learned that Tyler was bent on annexing Texas, he too resigned, and this gave the President an opportunity to name a Secretary more suited to his purposes, whom he readily found in Judge Abel P. Upshur, of Virginia, who was indeed devoted to this cause until his tragic death two years later.

After the rejection of Texas in 1837, all discussion of the subject had been dropped, and it was now necessary for the Tyler administration to re-open the question in some way. When Houston was inaugurated president in 1842, he extolled England as the ally and friend of Texas and warned his people to expect neither help nor sympathy from the States.

Secretary Upshur sent word to Houston in a guarded way that the Tyler administration would like to open negotiations for a treaty of annexation. But the old Cherokee chief feigned not to see or hear these overtures, and continued his open parleys with England, which were meeting with a warm and equally open response from the British statesmen who desired to control the destiny if not acquire the territory of Texas. Houston sent Doctor Ashabel Smith, of Goose Creek, as Minister to England and France. Smith, next to Houston, was the greatest mind of the Republic of Texas. England had a powerful influence with Mexico, and tendered its good offices to fix a truce between that country and Texas, and the hint was had that if Texas would stay clear of the States, Mexico might be induced to acknowledge Texas independence, and thus put a stop to the eternal guerrilla border warfare which had prevailed since 1836.

Even Mexico, anxious to forestall annexation by the States, lent color to this hope and an armistice for a time prevailed. Houston foresaw that if he appeared favorable to the new proposals of annexation, he would at once alienate English aid, and if Tyler should fail to carry the scheme through, Texas would be left feeble at home and friendless abroad. And though he desired annexation to his native land more devoutly than any other ambition in his long career, he frowned so coldly on Upshur's advances that the administration appealed to Jackson, then in retirement, to use his influence with Houston in favor of a treaty of annexation. Houston finally consented to open negotiations, provided assurances of aid against Mexico were given by the Tyler administration in the event the treaty should fail of ratification by the United States Senate.

Houston's caution was to a degree frustrated by the anxiety of his constituents, who, hearing of the overtures from the Washington government, and noting his ostensible indifference, demanded steps to facilitate the project so dear to the heart of all Texas. And though he managed to keep the situation well in hand, yet the Texas Congress in December, 1843, voted to authorize a treaty of annexation, and it was in fact concluded between diplomatic agents of Texas and the Washington government early in 1844. So closely had these proceedings been guarded in the United States that the treaty was signed before any widespread information regarding it had escaped there. Rumors had now and then been rife, and some American daily papers had published warnings, but no one took serious notice of a project which was generally regarded as gone beyond recall.

But Tyler's treaty must yet go before the senate of the United States, and like another president who followed him with another treaty even in our own day, he must deal with the American Senate.

TYLER AND TEXAS

The news of Tyler's treaty was soon out, and provoked a wild protest in the North and East. The storm center of this opposition was in and about Boston, one of whose daily papers railed at it as "The contemptible scheme of a poor, miserable traitor, temporarily acting as President of the United States, a scheme which would end in ruin, bloodshed and disunion. We will resist it...with the last drop of our blood."

Petitions were written, mass meetings held, and all through the northeast the spirit which had defeated it in 1837 was aroused for its doom in 1844. Even the gentle Quaker poet Whittier, the author of "Barefoot Boy" and

"Maud Muller," whose harmless rhymes we learned in childhood, took up his pen against us and wrote:

Like a lion growling low,
Like a night storm rising, slow,
Like the tread of unseen foe;

It is coming, it is nigh,
Stand your homes and altars by,
On your own free threshold die;

Freedom's soil hath only place
For a free and fearless race,
None for traitors false and base;

and many more stilted stanzas advertising our wickedness.

And the venerable John Quincy Adams rushed to his voluminous diary and wrote: "The treaty of annexation was this day sent to the Senate, and with it went the freedom of the human race."

But these screams from New England were met by some very plain talk from down South. "We had rather have Texas than New England," thundered a Tennessee congressman, and all through the South there was open talk of withdrawing from the North, annexing Texas and extending our territory to the Pacific. But the fear of England had been to a degree put in the hearts of many people in the North. It was told that the British planned to do the carrying for Texas exports, and was to have an entry there for all manufactured goods duty free; that the plan was to exclude all American manufactured articles from the Texas market. And while Garrison thundered *"That those who would befriend Texas would dethrone God,"* and John Quincy Adams saw the doom of the human race in the Texas treaty, these things, though terrible, were more or less intangible like the minister's day of judgment and eternal punishment, while the loss of a commercial advantage or an open market was a present real distress. The prospective wrath of God was not quite so terrible to a Yankee in those days as the immediate loss of a customer.

One petition sent to a congressman from Western New York declared in its preamble against the base iniquity of annexing Texas, but was accompanied by a postscript which advised that if their representative really believed England was about to take Texas, he was authorized to waive the iniquity and annex it.

At the beginning of 1844, the stage was set in the United States for the presidential campaign, and the country was thought to be closely divided between Democrats and Whigs. Four years before the Whigs had won, and this year they planned as they had often planned before and afterwards to renominate and elect Henry Clay, and "Lord Harry" was compelled to say something about Texas. Being a Southern man and having been one of the first to speak out for Texas in 1836, he was counted on by the administration to support the treaty. But he was destined to be neither right nor president in 1844, and he spoke out against it, and the Whig party turned its back on Texas. Van Buren had the pledges of twenty-one states, mostly Southern, for the Democratic nomination, and he planned to keep very silent on the Texas question, and he was a great master of the art of silence.

He lived so close to the roar of abolition and anti-annexation that he dared not speak for it. On the other hand, his principal hope for nomination and election lay in the South. All efforts to draw a statement from him were without avail for a time, when some of the Southern Democratic leaders laid a plan to "blow Van out of the water."

He was the protege of Jackson, who had made him president. The old warrior in retirement was the greatest single force in the Democratic party, and the great passion of his closing days was the annexation of Texas and the circumvention of England. These designing gentlemen who would *blow Van out of the water,"* betook themselves down to the Hermitage and got a strong letter from Ex-President Jackson outlining what the party and Van Buren should do. Unable to keep silent longer, Van Buren came forth with his statement, long, involved and pointless, but against annexation *at this time*. The treaty was sent to the Senate April 22, 1844, where it was doomed to remain for weary weeks.

The Whig Convention met on May 1st, and nominated Henry Clay. There was no discussion of the Texas question in the Convention. No mention of it in the platform. They shunned it as they would the plague. They were so afraid of it that they did not mention Oregon, which was much coveted in the Northern and Western states. A delegate from Mississippi tried to be heard upon the question, but was unable to get the eye or the ear of the presiding officer. Those near him in the hall hearing the drift of his remarks, silenced him in short order. "Surely you would not inject this ugly Texas question and injure Henry Clay," they said reproachfully, and he lapsed into silence.

It was now a foregone conclusion that the Texas Treaty would not pass the Senate.

Benton, who in 1836 had declared for Sam Houston the greatest military accomplishment since Marc Antony, was the spokesman for the Democratic majority, and the mouthpiece for Van Buren. He turned on the treaty and Texas with bitter venom.

A few days after the Whig Convention adjourned there was another convention, held in Baltimore, which nominated John Tyler for president on a purely Texas platform. It was made up of self-appointed delegates from all sections of the country. It now seemed sure that the Democrats would name Van Buren and denounce the treaty, and with both great parties opposed to it, Tyler hoped to get enough votes to throw the presidential choice into the House of Representatives, where it would be a free-for-all fight. With this situation prevailing, the Democratic National Convention met at Baltimore on the 27th of May, 1844.

THE FALL OF VAN BUREN

The Democratic National Convention which met at Baltimore in May, 1844, was the most remarkable one which had ever assembled during the fifty years of our national life. It was the first to name a "dark horse" candidate.

For twenty years Andrew Jackson had been the idol and leader of his party. At the end of his second term, he could have been nominated and elected again, but never considered such a course. It was the marvel of Europe that a man in power would voluntarily surrender it as he did. His mantle had fallen on Martin Van Buren, who was elected to succeed him in 1836, but was defeated for a second term in 1840.

But Van Buren had held the party together, and by shrewd management had all but assured his nomination in 1844. But for the sudden advent of the Texas question he would have been nominated.

The Democratic party had controlled the destiny of the country during its formative period, and had elected five out of eight partisan presidents. Under Jefferson, Louisiana had been acquired, and Monroe had added the Floridas. All the traditions of the party were in favor of an expansion and the mastery of North America. But Van Buren was a man of small calibre, and fear of the abolition press had bullied him into a declaration against the treaty, and against what had always been the policy of the party. He had more than a majority of delegates pledged to his support, most of the pledges having been given before Tyler had so cruelly thrust the Texas question upon both parties. But the Southern leaders had sworn a vow that he should not be chosen. The voice of the chaplain's opening prayer had hardly died away when some enterprising person moved that the convention adopt the two-thirds rule, and that no nomination be declared until the candidate received two-thirds of the votes cast.

The Southern delegates, instructed for Van Buren, voted for the adoption of this rule, for in it they saw his defeat, without bolting their instructions. The friends of Texas were now in the saddle, the convention was deadlocked, Van Buren was beaten, and the Southern delegates brought forth and nominated Ex-Governor James K. Polk, of Tennessee, who was known to be "whole hogged for Texas." The Democratic platform declared for the re-annexation of Texas and the acquisition of Oregon. George M. Dallas of Pennsylvania, was nominated for Vice-President.

The action of the Democratic Convention championing the cause of Texas at once notified the world that the issue was to be fought out in what President Wilson would have called a "great and solemn referendum."

But Tyler's treaty was still before the Senate, and it was yet in session. The Whigs had a majority of seven in that body, and on June 8th they defeated the treaty, a solid Whig vote of 28 out of 29 being cast against it seven Democrats, lead by Benton, voting with the Whigs. "We have killed the treaty (said Senator McDuffie, of South Carolina), but a ghost is sometimes more terrible than a living man." In the meantime a messenger whom Tyler had dispatched to Mexico for the purpose of offering to purchase any opposition which that country might have to annexation of Texas, returned with the information that that country was much stirred, and that no peace could be purchased if we should carry out these plans.

Santa Anna, who was again in power there, asked his congress for men and money to resist American aggression.

The presidential campaign in 1844 was not essentially different from campaigns we have known in our day. The Whigs accepted the gauge of battle with hope and ardor. On one side they cried: "Polk—Slavery and Texas," On the other: "Clay—Union and Liberty." A popular Whig cry was, "James K. Polk and George M. Dallas—One for the devil and the other for the gallows." Mass meetings were held in which Texas was represented upon Whig banners as a forbidding looking female dressed in mourning. Democratic meetings displayed banners picturing her a beautiful maiden in bridal robes. Poor Clay found himself in an unhappy situation. When he had come out so boldly against Texas early in the year, he knew that Van Buren, whom he supposed would be his opponent, would do likewise, and felt that there would be no issue between them, and they both felt that it would not be a party question.

Now he saw Van Buren overthrown and a Southern Democrat opposed to him declaring for Texas and Oregon. At heart Clay, himself a Southern man, was for annexation, and as the campaign progressed and the issue became doubtful, he wrote more letters, which made a bad matter worse, and let it be known: "That he had no *personal objection* to the acquisition of Texas;...that he would be glad to see it, could it be done without war with common consent and without dishonor."

The most powerful figure in the campaign was General Jackson, who, though old and feeble, held the acquisition of Texas as the last strong sentiment of his wonderful career.

Hatred of England had ever been a passion with him, and hostility to that country was the strongest single sentiment which the Democrats sounded up and down the length and breadth of the land. The old warrior sat in his home down in Tennessee and wrote letters day and night, wrote with a feeble, trembling hand, directed by the fire of a yet powerful mind. It is estimated that he wrote hundreds of autograph letters to Democratic leaders north and south, making suggestions, giving directions. In one letter: "Support the cause of Polk and Texas, let Tyler alone." In another—"I am too weak to write much more, but with my last word I warn you against England, for it will grab Texas, if Polk is defeated." Through Jackson's influence, President Tyler was induced to withdraw from the race and cast his strength to Polk.

Sam Houston had secretly and powerfully aided the issue by creating an atmosphere which seemed to verify Jackson's warnings against England.

Polk was elected by a popular majority of less than forty thousand votes. But defeat of the treaty in the Senate in preceding June had cast a great calm over Texas. We had turned from offers of British aid to accept annexation, and with the door shut in our face by the Senate, Texas was degraded before the world. At home credit sank to its lowest ebb. Annexation had been turned down so often by the American Congress that the Texas people did not accept the election of Polk as decisive. They yet feared that the United States Senate would never accept Texas; that Polk could do no more than Tyler had been able to do with a hostile Senate.

Mexico, angered at the turn of affairs, gave notice that hostilities were renewed, and Santa Anna began pretended preparations to wage a campaign upon Texas by land and by sea.

TYLER'S TRIUMPH

John Tyler was a man of great energy, and the "re-annexation of Texas" was the prime purpose of his administration. During the campaign of '44, he had withdrawn from the race and thrown his influence to Polk, and he accepted Polk's election as a victory for his great purpose.

When Congress met in December, one of the first things President Tyler did was to send in a strong message urging legislation for the admission of Texas, and with it he submitted data from Mexico, including the boast of Santa Anna that he was about to invade Texas and conduct a merciless campaign for its reconquest. Mexico had been angered and aroused by the election of Polk on a platform which declared for acquiring Texas, and sharp, bitter correspondence had passed between the two countries.

Then, too, Tyler had given his word to Houston in 1843 that if the treaty negotiated that year should fail, Texas should have the aid of the United States in the event Mexico renewed the war against Texas.

England was genuinely alarmed, and British papers were filled with warnings to that government against allowing the United States to acquire Texas. Whatever doubt may have existed about the fate of annexation, as far as the United States was concerned, was dissolved by the ill-timed and unwarranted attacks by the English press and the intrigues which England put on foot to block the union of Texas with the States. The London *Times* declared the election of Polk "was the triumph of all that was worst in American life, and that England and all Europe must resist the extension of the United States to the southwest. The London *Morning Post* exclaimed; "The Republican monster must be checked."

Many people throughout the United States and some of the leading journals were turned to annexation by these British indiscretions, which fulfilled to a degree the forebodings of General Jackson.

And while it seemed politic to allow the matter to await the inauguration of Polk, in March next, yet there was a general feeling that it was dangerous to wait.

A prominent Democratic congressman, speaking of Tyler's message, warned the country: "Let not procrastination be the thief of Texas." Resolutions for annexation were promptly introduced in both houses of Congress, and from December to February the battle in that forum was waged and won.

A resolution for annexation of Texas was offered and after passing the Senate and the House, it had President Tyler's signature on February 27, 1845, just five days before his term of office expired.

The fight in Congress was a spectacular one, and the galleries were thronged from day to day as the debates progressed.

Benton, who had fought the treaty so bitterly in June, found ground to support the cause in February. Its final passage was by a strictly party vote, the Whigs voting almost solidly against it. But there was a rift in the clouds of northern opposition, and most of the northern and eastern Democrats voted for it. The legislature of Ohio instructed its senators to support it.

The northern abolitionists received the result with ire and anguish, and Garrison, who in 1842 declared "That any one supporting Texas would dethrone God," now wrote in his Boston paper that the joint resolution of Congress "was a deed of perfidy as black as Egyptian darkness."

While the debates were proceeding in January and February, 1845, President-elect Polk came up to Washington from his home in Tennessee, and mingled with members of Congress, throwing the weight of his influence into the scale. "The pressure of two Presidents and an Ex-President is too much for us," exclaimed a Whig Senator.

The defeat of the treaty by the Senate in June had brought the Tyler administration face to face with its obligations to Texas, which had been exacted by President Houston in 1843 before he would negotiate the treaty. He had stipulated, and Tyler had promised, that in the event the Senate should fail to ratify the treaty and the negotiations should bring on war with Mexico, that the United States would aid Texas and guarantee her independence.

Tyler probably had no constitutional authority to make such a promise and less to perform it, nevertheless he acted promptly to make it good. On September 10, 1844, John C. Calhoun, Secretary of State, sent through Shannon, American Minister to Mexico, a most remarkable and vigorous paper which in terms warned Mexico to let Texas alone.

Calhoun advised that the rejection of the treaty by the Senate did not mean the abandonment of annexation, but that the United States intended to acquire Texas, and any invasion of Texas by Mexico pending these negotiations still pending would be resented by the United States; that the President had fully determined that Texas should not suffer at the hands of Mexico because of the recent overtures towards annexation.

"If Mexico has taken offense at these negotiations," said Mr. Calhoun, "it should attack the United States, as we are the ones who proposed annexation."

The loud threats of Mexico, which became louder after the November election, brought Tyler's promise to Houston into a present obligation, and was a cause for Tyler's urgency in submitting the Texas question in December instead of passing it over to Polk's administration, which would not begin until March.

There has been much criticism of Tyler and Polk for the war plans they carried on in the latter part of 1844, and during 1845. It has been written and millions believe that Polk without warrant provoked a war of conquest with Mexico. But when one remembers that Texas was a free country when Tyler began negotiations for annexation in 1843, and that he had given President Houston his promise that it should not suffer as the result of these negotiations if the treaty should fail, and when we see Mexico blustering with preparations for a merciless campaign against Texas because of these very negotiations, we are lead to reverence the memories of Tyler and Calhoun and Polk for the military preparations they began in 1844 and carried forward in '45 and '46, while the details of annexation were being worked out by both countries.

The greatest triumph in American history after the Revolution of 1776 was the prompt, powerful way the Tyler and Polk administrations moved to solidify Texas and put the flag over the country west to the Pacific.

The Activity of England

England had determined that Texas should not become part of the American Union, and hoped that Mexico would reconquer it, and long after all hope of this reconquest was obviously gone, it acknowledged Texas independence. The overwhelming defeat of annexation in the American Congress in 1837, and the loud roarings of the northern and eastern press misled England into the thought there was no chance that this country would ever accept Texas.

When Tyler's treaty of 1844 became known, there was an active and vigorous movement among English diplomats, and Lord Aberdeen sought an understanding with the French government that the two countries would join Mexico in preventing annexation. Guizot, the Prime Minister in the government of Louis Phillipe, seems to have committed his country to such a course, and if France had remained bound it is apparent that there would have been a world war if the United States had persisted in the course it did pursue.

But when it became known in France that the government had made such a commitment, there was an explosion such as can only happen in the French Chamber, and Guizot was denounced as the tool of England and for having turned on an old friend to serve the purposes of an ancient enemy. All hope that France would aid England by force of arms was gone, yet the government of Louis Phillipe did continue to give its moral support through diplomatic pressure to prevent annexation. But the British Minister at Washington forecasted the defeat of the Tyler treaty, and after the Democrat and Whig parties had named their candidates and made Texas an issue, Lord Aberdeen and his counselors wisely determined to lay low and await results. They knew that any British activity at this juncture would mean the defeat of Clay, and their ardent hope was for his election, which they thought would close the door to annexation. The election of Polk upset all their calculations.

When in December, 1844, Tyler again submitted the question to Congress, and it became evident that it was to be rushed to a conclusion, there was a great activity in the British Foreign Office, and a definite plan was at once worked out. It was well known in London as in Washington that what the people of Texas wanted above all things was peace and protection against Mexico, and a surcease of the ten long years of semi-warfare which prevailed. And so the English Ministry, bound to act in great haste, and bound to offer Texas some real inducement to stay out of the American Union, sought the seemingly hopeless task of inducing Mexico to acknowledge Texas independence and make a treaty of peace with Texas upon condition that it would not join the American Union.

This was indeed a bold plan, and one familiar with the Mexican history of this period will be struck with the height of British diplomatic audacity and daring. Since the campaign of 1836, it had been the hope by day and dream by night of all Mexico to reconquer Texas. Mexican officers who could not have been induced this side of the Rio Grande by any earthly consideration, were eternally swashbuckling up and down the tropics declaring that they would soon lead an army into Texas.

Every Mexican president or dictator who ruled his alloted day could raise large sums of money through the Mexican Congress for a campaign in Texas. Santa Anna, who was now and then in power during this period, 1836 to 1845, was always announcing vast plans for such, a campaign.

But the situation was desperate with the British Ministry, goaded on by an arrogant English press, which demanded that Texas be kept out of the American Union. A leading London journal declared in brutal British frankness, that Texas, in fact all North America, should be under a kind of British suzerainty. "*The Republican monster must be checked,"* and since France would not agree to an alliance to employ force, it must be done by cunning. While the Texas question was being debated in the American Congress in January and February, 1845, and when it was obvious that a resolution declaring for admission would pass, Almonte, the Mexican Minister to Washington, demanded his passports and let it be known that war would follow annexation.

When Terrell, Texas Minister to England and France, succeeding Dr. Smith, reached London in January, 1845, he was bluntly told that news had preceded him that the new president of Texas, Anson Jones, was an avowed advocate of annexation, and if so Texas need expect no aid from England in any of its problems.

Mr. Terrell hastened to correct this erroneous impression, and reported that thereafterwards a very different atmosphere prevailed, and he was given many kindly suggestions and offers of English aid which indeed were helpful, for as yet the American Congress had not passed the annexation resolution, and was still violently debating Tyler's December message.

DIPLOMATS GATHER ALONG THE BRAZOS

Foreseeing a shrewd diplomatic duel, and fully advised as to England's plans, President Tyler named Andrew Jackson Donelson, nephew of General Jackson, and a man of unusual force and sagacity, Charge to Texas.

The British government was and had for some years been represented in Texas by Charles Elliot, a former sea captain, who had been so long in the country as to be well acquainted with its people and its public men.

The French government was represented by an impetuous ass, Compte de Saligny, who had found Austin an uncomfortable place to live, and after quarreling with everybody in town, had removed to New Orleans, where he looked after French affairs in Texas at a long range.

In December, 1844, a few days before Tyler sent his last Texas message to Congress, Anson Jones became president of Texas. Although it was known that annexation would be offered Texas in a few months, he wisely made no mention of this ever-absorbing topic in his inaugural address. President Jones had seen annexation offered and snatched away too often to be over-sanguine at present prospects. Shortly after his inauguration he advised Captain Elliot that if Mexico could be brought to recognize the independence of Texas, he favored declining annexation, and he invited the British and French governments to interest themselves to that end. This was just what England hoped for. Congress had not then acted on Tyler's December message, nor did Jones know that the question had been put before the closing session of Tyler's last Congress. He supposed negotiations would await the inauguration of Polk. While these assurances were being given the British Representative, Ashabel Smith, Secretary of State in Texas, wrote the Texas charge at Washington "that the President Jones wished him to use his most strenuous exertions for annexation." When the news reached Galveston in the latter days of March, 1845, that Congress had passed and Tyler approved a plan for the annexation, Captain Elliot, and Compte de Saligny, hearing that Colonel Donnelson was on his way from Washington, D. C., to Washington on the Brazos, with an official communication from President Polk to President Jones, made great haste to Washington on the Brazos, which was for the time being the seat of Texas government.

Once there they went into a long conference with President Jones and Doctor Ashabel Smith, and urged many good reasons why Texas should remain independent.

President Jones advised them that while he personally thought Texas should remain a nation, yet he realized that the people of Texas desired annexation, and he saw in himself merely their agent.

After many conferences with his cabinet and *after taking the matter under advisement* for several days, he finally, on March 29th, tentatively agreed with the representatives of England and France upon the outline of a treaty which they were authorized to procure from Mexico:

1. Mexico consents to acknowledge the independence of Texas.
2. Texas will not annex herself to any country.
3. Boundaries to be fixed in final treaty or submitted to arbitration.

While these worthy diplomats were procuring these things to be done they exacted that for ninety days from date Texas would not enter into any negotiations for annexation. These things done, Captain Elliot agreed in furtherance of the plan to go at once to the City of Mexico, and he and the Compte de Saligny scampered down the Brazos, the Captain going incognito to Vera Cruz, and the Compte back to his well stocked wine cellar at New Orleans, each thinking he had overawed the President of Texas, and outwitted the President of the United States. On their way out of town they met Colonel Donnelson, the American Charge, who was hastening for an interview with President Jones, and to lay before him and the Texas Congress the plan of annexation.

It was known that the Texas Congress was overwhelmingly for annexation, and since the resolution of the American Congress only called for ratification by the Texas government, it was planned by President Jones and Doctor Smith not to call Congress in session until these envoys had an opportunity to try their hands in getting the Mexican treaty. President Jones hoped to be able to lay before Congress, when he assembled it, not only a plan for annexation, but the alternative of remaining an independent nation with a settlement of all troubles with Mexico, and this he did.

Colonel Donnelson did not find a congenial atmosphere

at Washington on the Brazos, when he arrived there on April 1, 1845, and laid the plan of annexation before President Jones and his cabinet. The President took the matter *under advisement*, for he said the gravity of the situation would not permit haste.

When Colonel Donnelson urged him to convene Congress, he said he had decided to lay it before the people through a convention to be called for that purpose.

Unable to get Jones to call Congress in session, Donnelson sought Ex-President Houston, whom he found at his home in Huntsville, and was much surprised to learn that he too was unfavorable to an acceptance of the resolution which had passed Congress in February. He did not think it fair to Texas, and pointed out some sharp objections to it, and proposed that negotiations between the two countries be begun and a treaty of annexation agreed upon. He favored a treaty because it could be abrogated at any time by either party, and one wonders what would have happened in 1861 had Texas come into the Union under such a treaty. But it was explained to Houston that President Polk and Secretary of State Buchanan did not think it wise to delay while negotiations would be going forward, and he withdrew his objections at least to the extent that he used no effort to frustrate Donnelson's plans, and took a trip to the Hermitage for a farewell to Jackson. Donnelson was not openly told, but indeed he heard it on the streets, that an "offer from Mexico" might be made at any time and that the Texas government was waiting for it.

In the meantime April was well advanced, and the people of Texas had become very impatient of delay, and very strong pressure was brought to bear on President Jones to convene Congress and all kinds of rumors were afloat as to his designs against annexation. In fact a plan was well on foot to convene Congress anyhow if he did not act, and the murmurings were so loud and the criticism of the government so great that the Mexican Consul at

New Orleans advised his government that a revolution was imminent in Texas.

Yielding to these importunities before he had time to hear from Captain Elliot, President Jones issued a proclamation on April 15, 1845, calling Congress to meet at Washington on the Brazos on June 16th. He calculated that this would give Elliot time to accomplish whatever could be done in Mexico. Doctor Jones' slow, calculating movements and Doctor Ashabel Smith's known views against annexation aroused much feeling in Texas in the spring of 1845, and the country was at a white heat as the hour approached for the extraordinary session of Congress in June.

CAPTAIN ELLIOT IN MEXICO

Captain Charles Elliot was not a great man, but he was an energetic one, and he had lost no time in getting from Washington on the Brazos to Galveston, where, by a fine coincidence, he found a British man-of-war at his disposal. He took passage on this vessel, giving it out that he was going to New Orleans, but was landed at Vera Cruz, from where he hastened on to the City of Mexico.

April, 1845, was an off season for Santa Anna, who was for the time being out of power and in exile (but he came back next year.) Herrera was, between revolutions, as it were, president ad interim of Mexico, and to him and his cabinet Captain Elliot, assisted by the British Minister to Mexico, addressed the proposition which he brought from the President of Texas.

It contemplated that Mexico would acknowledge Texas independence, upon condition that Texas would not join the American Union, boundaries to be settled later.

The proposition at first aroused great opposition at the Mexican capital. "Give up Texas, never," was the scream of Mexican papers and the wild boast of swashbuckling

Mexican military men. But the British envoys worked power fully on their fears. If they did not do this, Texas would be forced into the American Union for protection against the "great military force of Mexico." "The acquisition of Texas by the United States made that detested country the next door neighbor of Mexico, and an effort would follow to conquer and annex Mexico."

In proof of this the relators read from debates in the American Congress, where excited Whig leaders had openly charged that the Southern Democrats contemplated the extension of empire to Panama and the Pacific. And as confirmation of the perfidy of these Southern Democrats, if corroborations were necessary in the Mexican mind, they read and published the awful indictments brought against them by northern newspapers. These arguments were reinforced by Juan Nepomuceno Almonte, Mexican Minister to the United States, who had left Washington upon the passage of the Annexation Act in February.

Almonte, who was a man of great influence in Mexico, urged his government to accede to the British proposals, for he favored and impressed his people with the apprehension that the acquisition of Texas meant the conquest of Mexico by the United States of the North. This fear had foundation with Almonte, for he had been at San Jacinto. But it was an awful thing for the Mexican government to do: "Give up Texas to those mendicants who came to us and asked for land, and who forgot our kindness and bounty and turned traitor and brigand." How they suffered in the flesh as they struggled between this awful sacrifice and the fear of seeing all Mexico become an American dependency.

When the English diplomats pressed them to act, they professed a willingness to do so if England would guarantee Mexican sovereignty and the boundaries between Mexico and the United States, but just here there was a ant of zeal on the part of Her Majesty's representatives, for this meant war, and after France had withdrawn from the pact of Guizot, England was not willing to go to war alone. Finally the point was urged that Mexican honor was saved, since Texas was here suing for peace, and making a concession in order to get the boon of Mexican permission to live and be an independent nation.

While these conversations were going forward at the Mexican capital, news came late in April that President Jones had issued a call convening the Texas Congress in June. Captain Elliot knew full well what this meant, and knew that the only hope of defeating annexation lay in his returning to Texas at once with a treaty between Texas and Mexico ready to be presented for ratification when this Congress met.

Daily during April reports reached Mexico that the United States was sending war ships into the Gulf and was massing troops on the Texas frontier, and finally Elliot, and Bankhead, the British Minister to Mexico, succeeding in wringing and extracting an agreement from the Mexican Congress to make the Texas treaty in order to frustrate the designs of the United States. On the last day of May, 1845, Elliot was again in Galveston armed with the Mexican agreement to make a treaty acknowledging Texas independence on condition it would not unite with the United States. But all the diplomats in the world could not have accomplished the task that had been assigned this retired sea captain.

While President Jones hesitated and *took matters under advisement* and waited to hear from Elliot, things were happening in Texas.

Colonel A. J. Donnelson, nephew of Andrew Jackson and accredited representative of the United States in Texas, was a modest, quiet person, who moved with great celerity and acted with great accuracy. He knew where Colonel Elliot had gone and what he was doing, and he was in constant touch with the leaders of thought in Texas, and worked with them to stir public sentiment. He made great capital out of the intrigues of England, and exposed them to such men as Sidney Sherman, Edward Burleson, General Rusk and others who were working with him.

Colonel Elliot helped Donnelson by his free talk, seeing upon his return that the tide had set heavily against him. He talked loosely and wildly of coming trouble, and predicted dire disaster if Texas attempted to join the Union. He said that England and France would join Mexico in a war against the United States, and that Texas would be the battleground of a long, bloody world war.

Speaking as the accredited agent of England, many believed that he knew what he was talking about, and that grave trouble would follow. But the people who had come into the wilderness with Austin, and who had suffered the hardships of the quarter of a century which had intervened, could not be bullied, and the blustering talk of this retired sea captain, though he spoke as the envoy of the British Empire, carried little terror to the heart of the average Texan.

On May 5th, a few days after Elliot's return, President Jones issued a call for a general convention of the people of Texas at Austin on the fourth of the following July, "to consider the overture of the United States."

President Jones was abused and driven out of public life for what the people of Texas always believed to be his attitude towards annexation, and his willingness to form an alliance with England and Mexico against the United States.

But it must be remembered that he had seen the United States turn bitterly on Texas in 1837. He had witnessed the fate of the Tyler treaty in 1844, a treaty which the Washington government had sought and urged the people of Texas to make. No man foresaw just what would happen in the United States even as late as May and June, 1845. In January of that year James Reilly, sometimes our representative at Washington, wrote Jones: "Annexation is very much like the Millerite doctrine of the end of the world. It may be today, it may be next session, it may not be until the saints of this generation are all dead." Houston had said to Jones, shortly before the latter became President, that in dealing with this question the Texas government "Should be wise as lynxes and as sly as foxes."

Now Doctor Anson Jones, though a good man and a true patriot, was not an artist in the lynx-fox game. He lacked the training and much of the great ability of the old Cherokee Chief, and in all this dilemma he was trying to play Houston without Houston's ability or experience. He was not at home in a game of duplicity and diplomacy.

It was with a degree of pride and a consciousness of having done Texas a great service that President Jones made public announcement of the Mexican treaty in May. Here he gave his people the choice to remain an independent nation with high guaranties of territorial integrity, or to become associated with the Union. They were no longer driven to join the United States for peace and protection.

But the news, instead of being received in this spirit, roused a storm all over Texas which would have overthrown his government were it not for the fact that he had convened Congress to meet within less than thirty days.

THE LAST ACT OF THE GREAT DRAMA OF ANNEXATION

The Ninth Congress of the Republic of Texas met in extraordinary session at Washington on the Brazos on the 16th day of June, 1845, to consider the matter of annexation.

In his message President Jones laid before Congress the American proposition of annexation, and also the proposed Mexican treaty. The sentiment of the people of Texas will be well explained by the fact that annexation was accepted by the unanimous vote of both houses of Congress, and that the Mexican treaty was unanimously rejected. These things so promptly done, Congress gave sanction to President Jones' convention called to meet at Austin on the 4th of the following July, for it was necessary for the people of Texas to form a state constitution and set up a state government.

In justice to the memory of Anson Jones, and as a vindication of his caution and refusal to put absolute faith in the American overture of February, 1845, we should remember the fate of similar overtures during the last decade, and also it is worthy of note that even after Texas had accepted the last proposal and formed a state government, and presented its state constitution to the American Congress for ratification, there was an effort made in the United States to withdraw the offer and leave Texas with its federal government dismantled and statehood rejected. Such a result would have found it disorganized at home and friendless abroad, with Mexico's whole force marshaled on its borders, the very force which was hurled against the armies of the United States in the war which followed in a few months. The infamy of such course impairing and breaking the faith of the government of the United States with such awful consequences to Texas, is almost unbelievable to this generation, but, though sad, it is true that Horace Greeley advocated it in the New York *Tribune.* And when the Congress met in December, 1845, before whom the details of formal admission must come, memorials and petitions by the thousand were pouring in from Northern and Eastern states urging that Texas be not admitted. The legislatures of Massachusetts and two other New England states joined in this demand, and John Quincy Adams lead a fight for its rejection in the House, and even the great Webster voted against the measure when it passed the Senate in December, and he was joined in this vote by thirteen Senators.

The Extraordinary Session of the Ninth Congress of Texas adjourned after a short but harmonious session, leaving the further details to the July convention. In the interim news came of the death of Ex-President Jackson at his home, the Hermitage. He had played a powerful part in the history of Texas, as well as that of the United States. His anxiety to acquire Texas, dating back to his first administration in 1829, and his lifelong intimacy with Houston, have given color to rumors which will ever prevail that he had a secret understanding with Houston which aided to bring on the Revolution of 1836. His passion for annexation was intensified after his retirement by the discovery of British intrigues, for among the many ruling passions of his long life was his deep hatred for England. He was of Scotch ancestry, and during the American Revolution, when yet a mere lad, a British officer struck him a cruel blow for refusing to shine the officer's boots, and he carried a scar into international history.

The July convention ratified annexation with but one vote against it, and that was cast by Richard Bache of Galveston, a grandson of Benjamin Franklin. This convention formulated our constitution of 1845, which was submitted to the people of Texas in November, at which time it was ratified and at an election held in December, J. Pinckney Henderson was elected governor.

The constitution was then presented through President Polk to the American Congress, and in December, 1845, it formally admitted Texas into the Union.

On the 16th of February, 1846, the first Legislature of the State of Texas met at Austin, and President Jones formally closed the affairs of the Republic and surrendered his office to Governor Henderson. The Republic was born at Washington on the Brazos on March 2nd, 1836, and the span of its life was but two weeks less than ten years.

The annexation resolution passed by the American Congress, under which Texas was admitted, provided:

First: The State to be admitted subject to the adjustment by this government of all questions of boundary that may arise with other governments, and the constitution to be formed by Texas to be transmitted to the President of the United States to be presented to Congress on or before January 1, 1846.

Second: Said State, when admitted to the Union, after ceding to the United States all public edifices, fortifications, barracks, forts, harbors, navy and ship yards, etc., and all other means pertaining to the public defense belonging to said Republic, shall retain all the vacant lands lying within its limits to be applied to the payment of its debts. But in no event are said debts to become a charge upon the government of the United States.

Third: New States of convenient size not exceeding four in number in addition to said State of Texas and having sufficient population may hereafter by consent of said State be formed out of the territory thereof which shall be entitled to admission under the provisions of the Federal Constitution. Such States as may be formed out of the territory lying south of 36 degrees and 30 degrees, known-as the Missouri Compromise Line, shall be admitted into the Union, with or without slavery, as the people may desire. And in such States as may be formed out of said territory north of the Missouri Compromise Line, slavery shall be prohibited.

The boundaries between Texas and Mexico had never been fixed. The Republic had always claimed to the Rio Grande, and Santa Anna in his negotiations while a prisoner with us had agreed upon the Rio Grande as the boundary. If you will look at the map you will see that the Rio Grande rises in Colorado and flows south and east through New Mexico, leaving about half of the latter state to the east. The State of Texas claimed all of this territory, and it became the basis of a very bitter controversy between the state and federal governments during the Taylor administration in 1850. As a part of the celebrated compromise measures in 1850, the present northern and western boundaries were agreed upon, Texas surrendering all claims to New Mexico, but receiving for this concession ten million dollars, which was used to liquidate the debts of the Republic.

The annexation of Texas, accomplished in February, 1846, brought on a war with Mexico which began in the following April. The direct result of the war was the acquisition of all the country west of Texas to the Pacific.

The war with Mexico was not regarded with favor in the North and East, where the abolition leaders saw in it a scheme to extend slave territory. The poet Whittier, hearing of the terms of peace which the Polk administration would impose on Mexico, and that they would take the country west to the ocean, wrote a note of sympathy to the Mexican people, warning them that the invader was coming:

> *Let the Sacramento herdsmen heed*
> *what sound the Wind brings down,*
> *Of footsteps on the crisping snow,*
> *from cold Nevada's crown,*
> *Full hot and fast the Saxon rides,*
> *with rein of travel slack,*
> *And bending o'er his saddle leaves*
> *the sunrise at his back.*

Even so the Saxon came and snatched the great Southwest from the doom of the eternal anarchy which has prevailed south of the Rio Grande for these one hundred years.